THIRTY
DAYS
TO
MORE
POWERFUL
WRITING

THIRTY DAYS TO MORE POWERFUL WRITING

by

Jonathan Price

AVENEL BOOKS · NEW YORK

This 1982 edition is published by Avenel Books,
distributed by Crown Publishers, Inc.,
by arrangement with Fawcett Books

Manufactured in the United States of America

Library of Congress Cataloging in Publication Data

Price, Jonathan, 1941–
   Thirty days to more powerful writing.

   1. English language—Style.   2. English language—
Rhetoric. I. Title.
PE1421.P74   1982   808'.042   82-6770
                                     AACR2

ISBN: 0-517-385961

h g f e d c b

CONTENTS

6 Contents

INTRODUCING THE IDEA

What Is a Powerful Style?

A powerful style is your own. Not mine, yours. Not your high school composition teacher's—your own.

A powerful style is as flexible as you are; it should express your feelings and your thoughts as easily as you can when you talk at home.

A powerful style is as simple, or as complicated, as emotional, as exciting, or as intellectual as you want, depending on your aim and your audience.

A powerful style helps the reader understand you. Molière, the playwright most Frenchmen look to as their model of clarity, read his plays to his cook, to make sure every word made sense. Jonathan Swift checked the proofs of *Gulliver's Travels* with his servants, and changed any passage they did not immediately follow. When asked what style he aimed for, Daniel Defoe, the author of *Robinson Crusoe,* said: "I would answer, that style in which a man speaking to five hundred people, of all common and various capacities—idiots and lunatics excepted—should be understood by them all."

A powerful style moves people. Even the most factual writing can direct and subtly change our feelings. Strong political or religious writing can lead people into war, or reformation. And in a rally, a bold style can set people swaying, stomping, and yelling. Used without conscience, such a style can churn a crowd into a riot.

But such effects also depend on the writer's character—your character. To be clear, to be moving, your style must sound like you, not your lawyer. Michel de Montaigne, a mayor who had listened to far too many bureaucrats, said: "The talk I like is simple, even naive talk, on paper or out loud; juicy and nervous talk, short and clipped; not so refined and delicate, rather vehement and abrupt—not pedantic, not lawyerly, rather more soldierly." Like most people, he wanted to hear a real person, not just words.

Most people still write as they did in school, and their writing sounds that way—stiff, formal, fixed. Such writing is pompous, but not profound. It is fake. Oddly, honesty is a first step toward a more powerful style.

"A good style begins in the heart," said the eighteenth-century French writer Diderot, adding, "That is why so many women speak and write like angels, without having learned to speak or write, and that is why so many pedants will go on speaking and writing badly all their life, even if they go on studying, without learning." Your style, then, should be an image of your own character, but it will be only if you take the risk of paying attention to your real feelings, and your real aim in writing. Otherwise you will have nothing to say, and your words will be frosting on a cardboard cake.

Covering up your feelings, apologizing for your ideas, falsifying what you know, can make you sound fake. And outright lying will eventually ruin your style. Ezra Pound, a poet who saw money as a metaphor for poetry, said: "Any *general* statement is like a check drawn on a bank. Its value depends on what is there to meet it. If Mr. Rockefeller draws a check for a million dollars it is good. If I draw one for a million it is a joke, a hoax, it has no value."

But telling the truth is not that simple, at least when you start writing. You need techniques. At first, learning new techniques for writing may seem to slow down free expression. But when you have assimilated them, they will give you greater flexibility and free play. Pound also said, "The best work probably does pour forth, but it does so *after* the use of the medium has become 'second nature,' and the writer need no more think about *every detail* than Tilden needs to think about the position of every muscle in every stroke of his tennis. The force, the draw, follow the main intention, without damage to the unity of the act."

In this book, you will find thirty techniques for making your writing more personal, more striking, more alive. You will read examples of persuasive writing. If you just read these passages, you will get the idea. But, in order to develop your style, you should practice the techniques and do the exercises.

That takes work. But the work is made easier by two facts:
1. You are not learning someone else's style. You are actually just expanding and refining your own.
2. A powerful style depends on honestly stating your own feelings and ideas—and you already have experience doing that out loud.

Each chapter gives you a new way of saying things—a way you may already have used in ordinary conversation, but probably had not thought to apply to writing. Some techniques will appeal to you, some won't—that's your taste. Pick and choose what suits you, as you build your own style.

Most of the tricks of writing outlined in this book were "invented" when someone who was moved spoke that way spontaneously. Some listener noticed that the speech had a strong effect, thought about the way the words were arranged, and figured out "the technique." Each technique, then, is just a codification of what we sometimes do naturally when we speak. Knowing it consciously, practicing it on paper, getting it into our writing fingers, can help us bring some of our natural fluidity from talking into writing.

In thirty days you *can* change your writing style. It may take professional writers years to acquire a grand style. Thomas Wolfe, for instance, estimated that he had had to write a million words to polish his style. But you can get started in a month.

You have good reasons to change. Some are financial. The way you write may actually be costing you money. Some are personal. You may feel your own letters are lifeless. Or, if you have to speak in public, your style may be so awkward that your listeners lose track of your important points. At work, your memos may be so clumsy that your boss thinks you don't understand or can't explain what's going on. And when you answer a want ad, the awkward tone of your letter could lose the job for you.

Good writing can help you wake up your reader, teach people, woo someone. At mass meetings and in small groups, a strong style attracts attention; in memos and recommendations, your writing can win your department a contract, earn you a promotion, or defeat another's bad idea.

But the best reason for developing a more powerful style is to express yourself. When you say what you really mean, people listen. And when you make people feel what you feel, they applaud.

Remember, your audience wants to hear from you. Not from some robot. From a real human being—someone who makes jokes, someone who tells sad stories, outlines real ideas, thinks out loud, and is able to sum it all up in a quick phrase.

People look for a trace of your personality in everything you say and write. Through experience and exercise, you can learn to let your personality breathe its life and power into your style.

1st DAY

Beginning

Before you write, imagine you're finished. In your mind, finger the typed pages, look at the title, listen to your readers' reactions. Then think: who are these readers? What tone seems right for talking to them? And, basically, what's your main point?

Daydreaming the whole helps your mind come up with the necessary parts—the details, questions, references, half-recalled quotes, dimly remembered theories, and gut reactions—the raw data you'll turn into prose. Your picture of the final essay or story may be vague: that's normal.

As you write, you'll sharpen your vision of the final form; you'll discover proofs, and new ideas; you'll go beyond these fumbling attempts. Only when you've written your rough draft will you be able to come up with an appropriate first sentence. So don't worry the first sentence like a cat teasing a half-dead mouse. Write something and go on. You'll often find your true beginning three pages into the material.

Take a break, too. Clean your desk instead of sitting down to write. Rearrange your furniture, or sharpen a dozen pencils. Read the Bible, walk five miles, hum Mozart, mend a sock. Perform whatever rituals you habitually do before writing. But do them without guilt. The aim: to clear your brain of stray anxieties, shopping lists, irrelevant tugs on your attention.

And make sure you have enough time, after these preliminaries, to dawdle, doodle, and scratch notes without being interrupted. Think ahead: on an average day, when could you find a few hours free from phone calls, lovers, intruders? Fixing a definite time to write every day helps your mind prepare for the work—to gather ideas in the back of your consciousness, so that they are ready to surface when you're free. So make yourself comfortable, on a regular basis. By the way, have you had enough to eat? Are you relaxed?

When you're breathing slow and deep—that's the time to start writing down your first impressions. Nothing polished yet. Just whatever comes up.

SELF-DIAGNOSIS

When can you make time for writing, most days? ⎯⎯⎯⎯⎯⎯⎯⎯⎯⎯⎯

What rituals do you like to perform, before getting down to writing? ⎯⎯⎯⎯

_____

_____

_____

_____

List some writing projects you've thought of doing. _____

_____

_____

_____

Pick one of these, and imagine it's finished. What does it look like? How heavy is the manuscript? What praises come from your ideal readers—the ones who love you? (Ignore your critics for the moment.) _____

_____

_____

_____

_____

When you come to write what you *think* will be your opening, you'll find you face three tasks at once: telling the reader what you're going to write about, making that sound useful or interesting, and—hardest of all—suggesting your own view of the subject. Beginnings tease and announce. They lead us on, they let us see a glimpse of what's to come, while giving us reasons to read more.

Here are two introductions. Which do you find more intriguing?

> It is my purpose to consider the type of justification which is available for be- lief in the doctrines of religion. [Alfred North Whitehead, *Religion in the Making*.]

> I want to tell you about a real cowboy, what he is like, what his work is, and what it means. His name is Ralph Allan, and he came to Wyoming from New York City. [Fawn Deering, *Cowboys*.]

Both make their subjects clear. But Whitehead makes his dull. He has wor- ried the word *justification* until it lies dead in the sentence. Evidently he tried to sound neutral, even academic. He may have rejected the idea of starting out with the question he implies here: How can we justify believing in religious doc- trine? That might sound as if he opposed belief—violating his "objective" stance. But by stating his purpose so flatly, he manages to keep out any hint of his personal conclusions. Hasn't he considered these justifications already? Why is he involved? Where does he stand?

The *more* you reveal your position, the easier it is for the reader to decide if he likes you, and if he wants to read more. And he is likely to read on *if* you let your emotions show, even if they annoy him. Here are two other first sentences. Consider the author's emotional attitude toward Pilate, and Her, and ponder whether you would read on.

> "What is truth?" said jesting Pilate, and would not stay for an answer. [Francis Bacon, "Of Truth"]

> "To Sherlock Holmes she is always *the* woman." [Arthur Conan Doyle, "A Scandal in Bohemia"]

Bacon's anger at Pilate strikes us right off. And Arthur Conan Doyle's awe at *the* woman intrigues us. How did she impress the great detective so much? And why does Bacon state his subject, truth, with such emotion?

Such questions, aroused at the start, often incline a reader to go on because, by *suggesting*, but not spelling out, the author's emotional attitude toward his subject, they startle us—draw our attention—and make us wonder. So we continue on down the page.

FIVE ESSAYS

Imagine you have five essays to write by tomorrow morning, on the topics listed here. Write the first sentence of each, summarizing your own view of the subject with enough gusto to make your reader wonder about you.

Tomatoes: _____

_____

High Culture: _____

_____

Assassinations: _____

_____

Physical Exercise: _____

_____

Automobile Exhaust: _____

_____

Having surprised—maybe even fascinated—your reader, you have a grace period during which he will give you some attention while you get the main ideas moving. Don't waste his patience on apologies for your incompetence or throat clearing. Don't edge up to the subject like a swimmer dipping a toe. Skip the delaying tactics.

Plunge in. Dive into a mystery, or swim straight for your target. Either way, you get wet. You grapple with your subject right off. We can tell *how* you swim, and what you think is important. Just finding out this kind of information early inspires us with confidence. We feel you won't dillydally around. You respect our time, and you home in on the essential issues without embarrassment. (Who wants to reassure a hesitant writer?)

If you choose the straightforward plunge, you might quickly mention each topic you'll cover, in one paragraph. In this way, you provide the reader with a capsule outline of the whole work—and argue your case in miniature. When John Keats asked the question, "Why do new cars cost so much?" he found dozens of answers. So he invented a hypothetical consumer, Tom Wretch, and started his chapter by pointing out all the hidden, built-in charges behind the price tag Tom had just paid—thus previewing the topics that the rest of his chapter would cover:

> Ask Tom Wretch how much his new car cost, and he'll tell you what he paid for it. Ask him what his car is worth, and he'll give you the same figure. Tom means well, and he has answered you as best he can, but price, cost, and value are seldom synonymous, and nowhere is this truism more apparent than in the automobile business. Besides, Tom had no way of knowing that the price of his Stylepack Super included charges for tools he would never see or use, slipcovers never installed on his or anyone's car, railroad freight charges never paid to any railroad, magazines no one read, diamond rings, manufacturer's mistakes and taxes. Indeed, nearly two-thirds of the price Tom paid went for things other than the cost of the materials and labor that built the car, and some of these extra things were downright esoteric—Indian headdresses, for instance. [*The Insolent Chariots.*]

FAST PARAGRAPH

Imagine you are writing an essay about your feelings when you move at high speeds. Then write a paragraph outlining *in order* the experiences you would later devote whole paragraphs to.

_____

_____

_____

_____

_____

_____

_____

_____

_____

_____

_____

Or you can take a leap in the dark—sketching out some impenetrable mystery you intend to clear up; raising a question you will answer; or bringing up a problem you will solve. James Thurber, for instance, begins "University Days" this way: "I passed all the other courses that I took at my university, but I could never pass botany." Immediately we want to know: why not botany?

In his book about management, Robert Townsend begins one section with bold type: "**Campus Recruiting:** Send the people who can't go." We read on to find he wants to fire all campus recruiters, and send the most active managers out to talk to students. How come? Why would they be better? To find out, we must turn the page.

In the first paragraph of Ian Hunter's book on memory, the author denies that there is any such thing, piquing our curiosity:

> In everyday speech, we talk of having a good memory, of having a poor memory, of having a better memory for faces than for names, of having a memory that is failing, and so on. Such talk suggests that memory is an object, a thing which we possess in the same way as we possess a head or a big toe. Yet it is true, although alarming, to say that there is no such thing as memory. [*Memory*.]

Others begin with an apparent contradiction, encouraging us to read more, to see that paradox resolved. For instance, in *Curtains* Kenneth Tynan started one play review like this: "The most characteristic English play on the subject of physical love is Shakespeare's *Antony and Cleopatra*. It is characteristic because it has no love scenes." What? Well, how can it be about physical love, then? Tynan has held out the possibility that he and Shakespeare will discuss sex, while intriguing us by saying that Shakespeare does not *show* any physical lovemaking on stage.

A clearly stated paradox can introduce your concerns, while at the same time encouraging the reader to come up with his or her own solutions, and to check their hypotheses against your own. You provoke reading.

GREASE

Suppose that grease is your subject. Write the opening sentences for two essays, one viewing grease as a problem, the other viewing it as a surprising paradox.

1. The Problem of Grease: _____

_____

_____

2. The Paradox of Grease: _____

_____

_____

No matter what you write at the top of page one, go on. Later you may cross it out or save it. But you won't be able to judge your own first paragraphs until you've completed a run-through of the whole paper. Think of writing as a way of discovering more of what you think—not freezing it. And whether you outline your sequence of ideas, your method of attack, or a difficulty that your essay will clear up, keep on writing.

When to stop? Ernest Hemingway liked to stop each day's writing whenever he got to a scene he could imagine beforehand. That way, when he came back to his novel the next day, he already saw ahead, and he could start to work again, pausing only to reread what he had done the day before. So when you're just starting a long project, knock off while you can almost taste what comes next.

Remember, every day, before you pick up a pen,

- Make time.
- Get calm.
- Visualize the whole project.

And when you begin writing,

- Surprise us.
- Don't stall.
- State your subject early.
- Make your point fast.
- Outline your plan or method.
- Show what problem you'll solve.
- Keep on going.

THREE BEGINNINGS

IN the beginning was the Word, and the Word was with God, and the Word was God. [*The Gospel According to St. John*, King James version, I:i]

CALL me Ishmael. Some years ago—never mind how long precisely—having little or no money in my purse, and nothing particular to interest me on shore, I thought I would sail about a little and see the watery part of the world. It is a way I have of driving off the spleen and regulating the circulation. Whenever I find myself growing grim about the mouth; whenever it is a damp, drizzly November in my soul; whenever I find myself involuntarily pausing before coffin warehouses, and bringing up the rear of every funeral I meet; and especially whenever my hypos get such an upper hand of me that it requires a strong moral principle to prevent me from deliberately stepping into the street, and methodically knocking people's hats off—then, I account it high time to get to sea as soon as I can. This is my substitute for pistol and ball. With a philosophical flourish Cato throws himself upon his sword; I quietly take to the ship. There is nothing surprising in this. If they but knew it, almost all men in their degree, some time or other, cherish very nearly the same feelings towards the ocean with me. [Herman Melville, *Moby Dick*.]

WE, the people of the United States, in order to form a more perfect union, establish justice, insure domestic tranquility, provide for the common defence, promote the general welfare, and secure the blessings of liberty to ourselves and our posterity, do ordain and establish this constitution for the United States of America. [Preamble, U.S. Constitution]

2nd DAY

Getting Concrete

Whenever I start taking notes, my ideas seem hazy, my subject seems blurred. I begin in a fog.

As I write, my reactions become clear; I see where I am going. What seemed at first a vague landscape now becomes concrete. My subject takes on a particular color, and size, and shape, and texture. Shakespeare says that writers give to "airy nothings" a local address and a name. And a major part of the process of writing demands just that movement of mind—from the general to the detailed, from the abstract to the particular.

Be precise! It takes effort. It takes training. But this rule is so important that it underlies a dozen others.

How can you tell if something you've written in your first draft is still vague? Look for these symptoms:

- Big words clump up in bunches.
- Abstractions outnumber words describing real objects or acts.
- You cannot "see" anything—or hear it, or smell it.
- You could not draw a map, or set up a timetable for what goes on.
- You cannot find any real, easy-to-grasp examples of the general argument.
- In fact, everything is "in general"—nothing in such writing happens just once, in one particular place, to one particular person.

If you feel your own writing sometimes goes fuzzy, look into your motives as you write. For instance, if you were writing about the way Americans spend money, you might really think this:

> We buy clothes to show off, not to keep warm. We feel shabby when we are not "well dressed," and, even if we have to spend our food or rent money to do so, we dress up. Fashion, not function, sells clothes.

Now, what could possibly have motivated Thorstein Veblen to say that the way he did in the following paragraph?

> No one finds difficulty in assenting to the commonplace that the greater part of the expenditure incurred by all classes for apparel is incurred for the sake

18

of respectable appearance rather than for the protection of the person. And probably at no other point is the sense of shabbiness so keenly felt as it is if we fall short of the standard set by social usage in this matter of dress. It is true of dress in even a higher degree than of most other items of consumption, that people will undergo a very considerable degree of privation in the comforts or the necessaries of life in order to afford what is considered a decent amount of wasteful consumption; so that it is by no means an uncommon occurrence, in an inclement climate for people to go ill clad in order to appear well dressed. And the commercial value of the goods used for clothing in any modern community is made up to a much larger extent of the fashionableness, the reputability of the goods, than of the mechanical service which they render in clothing the person of the wearer. [*The Theory of the Leisure Class.*]

Perhaps we stay vague when we want to sound important, authoritative, or sophisticated. We talk around the point when we sense the reader would not agree. We moon dreamily about passion when we want to avoid mentioning names. The poet Swinburne often used the same word to describe a woman and a sunset: perhaps he was just lazy. We sometimes seize on a cliche, or a phrase of jargon, because it seems to say a lot without demanding that we think. Or we pick up a big word like a fishnet, hoping to catch twenty meanings (one ours, nineteen those of our confused readers). Precision is harpooning the one word we really want.

So imprecision starts when we do not know what we are talking about—or when for some reason we do not want to admit what we really mean. Ignorance is easier to cure. But lying, or covering up, or pretending, or boasting, or putting up a front—that is much more difficult to overcome. "The great enemy of clear language is insincerity," says George Orwell, the Englishman who wrote *1984*. "When there is a gap between one's real and one's declared aims, one turns as it were instinctively to long words and exhausted idioms, like a cuttlefish squirting out ink."

When we read Veblen, we notice all that ink is not saying much. We may be impressed, but we are not convinced. We may see just words, and dislike the writer; we may get a shaky idea of what he means, underneath, but we may still resent his putting it that way. Therefore, if Veblen wanted us to bow down to his authority, he succeeded; but if he wanted to persuade us, or to make something clear, he did not.

Vague talk makes listeners angry. On the other hand, concrete writing wakes up our senses. We seem to see what is being talked about; we can almost smell it. Our body responds and, given something real to think about, our mind shifts into alert. Such writing can move us, persuade us, make us argue.

FURNITURE

Let's start with a real object, a piece of furniture at home—something you cannot see right now.

What color is it? _____

What materials? _____

What textures? _____

What size? _____

What type? _____

Now put that all together as a series of adjectives piled up in front of the noun—the crudest way of describing.

_____

_____

What one detail distinguishes your table or bed from all the others manufactured in that lot?

_____

_____

_____

Notice how your description became more and more detailed as you recalled each aspect of that furniture. Some details may have seemed uncertain, in memory. That's normal. Some people have photographic recall; but most writers have to train their minds to record this kind of data, for later use. When Thomas Wolfe went to Europe, he felt homesick, and his memory brought back the pictures of life in the U.S.A. with miraculous clarity: "Suddenly I would remember the iron railing that goes along the boardwalk at Atlantic City. I could see it instantly just the way it was, the heavy iron pipes; its raw, galvanized look; the way the joints were fitted together. It was all so vivid and concrete that I could feel my hand upon it and know the exact dimensions, its size and weight and shape." [*The Story of a Novel.*]

LOOKING AROUND YOU

Since most of us do not exercise our memories much, we may need to train them by taking conscious notes. Look at a piece of furniture that's right in the room with you. Answer these questions as accurately as you can:

What kind of furniture is it? _____

What's on top of it? _____

_____

_____

Under it? _____

_____

_____

What colors does it have? _____

_____

What is it made of? _____

_____

How does it feel to the touch? _____

_____

_____

Does it have a smell? _____

How big is it? _____

How does it sound when you hit it? _____

How much material lies behind a simple word like *wastebasket!* And yet, trained by schools and bosses, bureaucrats call a wastebasket a "portable disposal system."

EATING WITH FIVE SENSES

Get something to eat. But before you eat it, describe it. What color is it? How does it smell, feel, sound? What different tastes show up as you chew, then swallow?

_____

_____

_____

_____

_____

The more sense impressions you evoke, the stronger we will "feel" the thing you are talking about. In the next exercise, think of some tourist site you've enjoyed. In one paragraph, reconstruct that experience, consciously appealing to all five senses. Make us smell it, hear it, taste it, see it, touch it.

_____

_____

_____

_____

_____

Movement signals life. Think about the descriptions you have written. Have you moved through the tourist area in the same direction as when you were there, noting first the parking lot, then the walkways, then the view itself? If so, you have helped the reader go through the experience as you had it.

A static description tends to lie flat. Keep it moving. Picking words that suggest activity—what you did, what went on, what other people did—also helps a reader imagine using the chair, handling the food, poking around on the sightseeing platform.

CHEWING YOUR PENCIL

Contemplate your pen or pencil for a moment. Where do you carry it? How do you hold it? When you write, how do you sit? What does it sound like on the paper? What else do you do with it?

You face a problem of order. Which activities should you mention first, which next? Figure out some sequence of actions that seems natural to you—you and your pen. Try not to be mechanical (first, second, third): say what you really think and do. A reader should come away from your paragraph with a sense of your tastes, habits, your way of handling such an apparently simple thing as a pen or pencil.

_____

_____

_____

_____

_____

_____

_____

The more observations you let slip about your life with your writing instrument, the more the reader picks up about you. In fact, one reason many people do not describe whatever they are talking about in detail is that they hesitate to reveal their own attitudes, and their way of looking at the world. The most revealing technique for ordering the flow of impressions is also the most subjective: you start with what really strikes you first (not what you later feel is most important), and then you proceed step by step, as your original impression grows. School trains you to ignore all of this for the conclusion, the upshot. But the more you write, the more useful this technique will seem. It allows a reader into your mind. A beginner joins another first-timer, to move through an experience neither has had before; the same questions come up; the same surprises occur; the same discoveries hit.

Following your own moment-to-moment impressions of anything takes effort. We are not trained to do it in school or on the job. So at first the mind rebels, offering either too many ideas at once or a blank.

Try this experiment. Close your eyes. Reach out and touch anything. Now what strikes you first about it? And then? And then? Follow your experience moment to moment, inside and out, mentioning what you see, what you hear, what you imagine in your mind, what your body feels. This skill does not just happen; it takes regular practice. Every day, for years. But we have each had experiences that we can recall with this intense particularity: an accident, or a time of extreme physical danger, or emotional shock. And physical detail, offered in more or less the order it makes an impact on your mind, can move a reader more, emotionally, than any abstract summary.

Thus, even if you are writing a report or an essay—something that must come to general conclusions—you can strengthen its emotional charge by using concrete examples. Charles Dickens, for instance, wanted to show that David Copperfield's schoolroom was forlorn and desolate. So he made a general statement first, then followed it up with an active tour.

> I gazed upon the schoolroom into which he took me as the most forlorn and desolate place I had ever seen. I see it now. A long room, with three long rows of desks, and six of forms, and bristling all round with pegs for hats and slates. Scraps of old copy-books and exercises litter the dirty floor. Some silkworms' houses, made of the same materials, are scattered over the desks. Two miserable little white mice, left behind by their owner, are running up and down in a fusty castle made of pasteboard and wire, looking in all the corners with their red eyes for anything to eat. A bird, in a cage very little bigger than himself, makes a mournful rattle now and then in hopping on his perch, two inches high, or dropping from it; but neither sings nor chirps. There is a strange unwholesome smell upon the room, like mildewed corduroys, sweet apples wanting air, and rotten books. There could not well be more ink splashed about it, if it had been roofless from its first construction, and the skies had rained, snowed, hailed, and blown ink through the varying seasons of the year. [*David Copperfield*.]

Some cautions: when you are writing along at full speed, you may think it a hindrance to stop and think for a second what color an object is. But remember that even a tidbit of physical fact helps a reader imagine the original object. Pause to be precise.

Also, when you do decide to describe a scene at length, you may slip into telling us about what usually happens, what almost everyone always does. As e.e. cummings says, I never met a man named Mr. Everyone. *Always* may be eternal, but since that means day and night, a reader is left in no particular time of day, wandering "all over," with a bunch of faceless "everybodies." Lists of plurals have the same bland effect, as when Thomas Gray saw a certain harbor: "... and all around it palaces and churches peeping over one another's heads, gardens, and marble terraces full of orange and cypress trees, fountains and trellisworks covered with vines, which altogether compose the grandest of theaters." *In general* is never as strong as *in particular*.

REWRITE

Rewrite these dull descriptions. First cross out *always, everyone,* and *everywhere*. Say when, who, and where. Ax *would usually* and make the person do it once clearly. When he handles an object, make sure we know what it looked like; and if he hits a chair, tell us what kind: He would always go into the big room where everyone sat and ate dinner. He would always see papers everywhere. He would sit down usually and read something, listening to everyone. He was always aware of the clock. Then he would usually eat his dessert.

_____

_____

_____

_____

_____

The leader had lost control of everyone. Everyone sat around talking. Some would smoke cigarettes, and some would eat food. No one would listen. He would say something or other, and then everywhere all you could hear was just everyone talking and talking.

_____

_____

_____

_____

_____

When we begin writing, we may be in the same fix Mark Twain was in when he got a job as a reporter for the Virginia City, Nevada, newspaper, during the gold rush years. He scurried around town trying to find something to fill up the columns; he needed events, people, details. Imagine his delight when a desperado shot a man in a local saloon that afternoon! Few of us have his luck, though. So you will have to add your own excitement.

Why be concrete?

- To liven up an abstract discussion.
- To convince the reader that you have been there, have looked at what you are talking about, know it.
- To take the reader there, imaginatively.
- To move the reader.
- To tell the truth.

And how?

- Avoid _would, always, everyone,_ and _everywhere._
- Move from a whole class to one particular object, event, or person.
- Report what you saw and felt from moment to moment.
- Make it move.
- Use all six senses.

MORE EXAMPLES

THE earth bursts before us. It rains clods. I feel a smack. My sleeve is torn away by a splinter. I shut my fist. No pain. Still that does not reassure me; wounds don't hurt till afterwards. I feel the arm all over. It is grazed but sound.

Now a crack on the skull, I begin to lose consciousness. Like lightning the thought comes to me: Don't faint, sink down in the black broth and immediately come up to the top again. A splinter splashes into my helmet, but has travelled so far that it does not go through. I wipe the mud out of my eyes. A hole is torn up in front of me. Shells hardly ever land in the same hole twice; I'll get into it. With one bound, I fling myself down and lie on the earth as flat as a fish; there it whistles again, quickly I crouch together, claw for cover, feel something on the left, shove in beside it, it gives way, I groan, the earth leaps, the blast thunders in my ears, I creep under the yielding thing, cover myself with it, draw it over me, it is wood, cloth, cover, cover, miserable cover against the whizzing splinters.

I open my eyes—my fingers grasp a sleeve, an arm. A wounded man? I yell to him—no answer—a dead man. My hand gropes farther, splinters of wood—now I remember again that we are lying in the graveyard. [Erich Maria Remarque, *All Quiet on the Western Front.*]

I CAN never forget my first day's experience as a reporter. I wandered about town questioning everybody, boring everybody, and finding out that nobody knew anything. At the end of five hours my notebook was still barren. I spoke to Mr. Goodman. He said:

"Dan used to make a good thing out of the hay wagons in a dry time when there were no fires or inquests. Are there no hay wagons in from the Truckee? If there are, you might speak of the renewed activity and all that sort of thing, in the hay business, you know. It isn't sensational, or exciting, but it fills up and looks business like."

I canvassed the city again and found one wretched old hay truck dragging in from the country. But I made affluent use of it. I multiplied it by sixteen, brought it into town from sixteen different directions, made sixteen separate items out of it, and got up such another sweat about hay as Virginia City had never seen in the world before.

This was encouraging. Two nonpareil columns had to be filled, and I was getting along. Presently, when things began to look dismal again, a desperado killed a man in a saloon, and joy returned once more. I never was so glad over any mere trifle before in my life. I said to the murderer:

"Sir, you are a stranger to me, but you have done me a kindness this day which I can never forget. If whole years of gratitude can be to you any slight compensation, they shall be yours. I was in trouble and you have relieved me nobly and at a time when all seemed dark and drear. Count me your friend from this time forth, for I am not a man to forget a favor."

If I did not really say that to him I at least felt a sort of itching desire to do it. I wrote up the murder with a hungry attention to details, and when it was finished, experienced but one regret—namely, that they had not hanged my benefactor on the spot, so that I could work him up, too. [Mark Twain, *Roughing It.*]

T O Clifton House on the Canadian came a lone rider on a long-legged buckskin. He was a green-eyed man wearing a flat-crowned, flat-brimmed black hat, black shirt and chaps. The Barlow & Sanderson Stage had just pulled in when the rider came out of the lava country, skirting the foothills of the Sangre de Cristos.

He was riding easy when they first saw him but his horse was dust-coated and the sweat had dried on him. The man had a tear in his shirt sleeve and a bloody bandage on his side. He rode directly to the stable and dismounted, caring first for his horse.

Only then did he turn and glance toward the house. He wore two tied-down guns. Pulling his hat lower he crossed the hard-packed earth and entered the house. "I could use some grub," he said, "a meal now and supplies to go." [Louis L'Amour, *Kilkenny.*]

3rd DAY

Describing a Person

The more a writer talks about people, the more people like to read what he has written. It's human.

We like gossip. When we catch sight of a real person, even on paper, our attention perks up. Our emotions begin to move; our thoughts grow sharper when we can think about a real person, rather than an abstract Mr. Average. And when we get some sense of what a writer thinks about the people he meets, we can gauge him as a person. Thus the writer who includes quick personal sketches of real people stops being an impersonal authority, and becomes simply human.

But in certain writing—scientific reports, say—we have been trained not to mention personalities, or at least not to say anything interesting about them. And we know that whenever we say something accurate about another human being, we give away what we are like. So even in personnel evaluations, fitness reports, personal recommendations, we tend not to say anything too precise. The result, though, is writing that sounds somehow false: neutral, perhaps, but dead as stainless steel.

Mentioning people, describing them in detail, sketching them quickly, even attacking them, strengthens your writing. Why?

1. It reveals your own taste and personality.
2. It suggests you are aware of other people.
3. People are more interesting than ideas.
4. When we can picture the people involved, we find it easier to think about the rest of the situation.
5. Our emotions are more easily aroused by people than by statistics.

We can mention people in passing, sketching just enough of their face or posture or dress to give the reader an impression. Or we can probe more deeply, as we make notes, asking ourselves the hundred and one questions a novelist must ponder as he invents a character. To organize this rich information, to condense it, and to give it meaning, we may seize on one dominant image of the person: either a visual picture of him or her doing something, or an analogy (he resembles a bear). Or we may subordinate our picture of the individual to our main argument, making the person simply an example. But if we mention a person over

27

and over, we may want to go beyond labels and images, suggesting a new side to him or her each time, thus letting the readers feel they are getting to know a three-dimensional human being who grows, changes, and develops.

EXERCISE

Since we learn so much from a person's face and eyes, we might start our quick takes there. Try describing the eyes of half a dozen people, some of whom you like, and some not. Use at least one adjective that suggests the color, and another that suggests the emotions underneath.

1. _____
2. _____
3. _____
4. _____
5. _____
6. _____

Another snapshot of someone at work: how does the person organize the workspace? Is it a mess? Is it too clean? Are the necessary tools there? Whether the person works in a kitchen, an office, or a garage, think concretely: what phrases best describe the place—and, by implication, the person?

_____

_____

_____

_____

Dress tells us a person's class, pride, taste, respect, age; clothes shorthand identity. Think of two different people, and thumbnail the difference just by listing their habitual costumes.

A wears _____

_____

B wears _____

_____

Think how much you *could* say about almost anyone you know well. You have detailed memories of their body, their clothes, their environment, their way of moving, talking, thinking, working, playing, eating. We do not usually put this information into words, but we have it. Prove this to yourself by thinking of the answers to the following questions. To write down the answers might take hours; but within a few seconds you can conjure up the visual images needed, if you know the person well.

- What does he like to do with his hands?
- What physical work does he do?

- What sports?
- How strong is he?
- What does his voice sound like?
- How does he smell?
- What is his favorite place to sit?
- What hobbies does he have?
- Does he make his own meals?
- What does he like to eat?
- How does he usually eat?
- What does his bed look like?

Such questions ignore the external descriptions of height, weight, skin color, age, hair, and sex—the raw data needed by police to spot a criminal. But how much more information comes up when you remember the actual scenes. And think of crucial moments in the person's life, major decisions, loves, jobs. A playwright often has to write hundreds of pages of background on a character, articulating this kind of data about a person who never existed, so that he can make that character seem real. When you write, the more this data slips into your work, the more we can sense, see, and almost touch that person.

Whenever your writing requires that you talk at length about someone, or refer to them over and over, you face a choice. One strategy is simply to label a person as one thing, and then repeat that description every time his name comes up. That way, the reader always recognizes him, but never learns any more. Like a bit part in a movie, such a "character" never grows on us.

Or you can move beyond labels. Ponder contradictions. Think back to the different pictures you have of the person you picked to answer questions about: the more interesting the person, the more varied the tastes and tendencies. The same man may like chopping trees down and sewing. The same woman may eat whipped cream and diet bars. A secretary who at first glance seems efficient may turn out to be causing problems for everyone else. Or the doctor who moves slowly may diagnose her patient's problems fast.

Personality often leaps out at us from the chinks in the ideal, from the gaps between habitual patterns of behavior. Wherever we are not strictly consistent, our life shows. Therefore, you may want to develop a sequence of not entirely consistent attitudes toward a person, as you go along, trying to figure out a larger, more comprehensive description.

EXERCISE

Take a person you know through work, someone you have changed your opinion of over time. What was your first impression? _____

What did you think later? _____

And what is your current opinion? _____

Of course, once you begin to hint at what is unique, and even self-contradictory, about a person, you will need a way to organize this information. How can we fit together these different impressions?

One of the best ways to sum up people, without knocking off too many of their rough edges, is to compare them to something else. The person we love may seem like a fire, an ocean, a storm, a forest. Someone we hate may strike us as an icicle, or a knife. When we choose a central picture of the person, we need an image large enough, and ambiguous enough, to accommodate all of our meanings.

For instance, Raymond Chandler, in *The Big Sleep,* spoke of a maid this way: "She looked like a nice old horse that had been turned out to pasture after long service."

Dorothy Parker once described a starlet as "The original good time who was had by all."

And here is John D. MacDonald's description of an actress: "With her head slightly bowed, looking up at me through her lashes, the gold-red weight of hair at the right side of her face had swung slightly forward. Suddenly I knew what she reminded me of. A vixen. A quick red fox. I had seen one in heat long ago on an Adirondack morning in spring, pacing along well in front of the dog fox with a very alert and springy movement, tail curled high, turning to see if he still followed, tongue lolling from between her doggy grin." [*The Quick Red Fox.*]

EXERCISE

Think of two people in authority, preferably ones you don't much like. Imagine what nonhuman but living things they resemble: animal, plant, fish, snake, bird, or bug. Mention at least two specific characteristics that would show a reader why that comparison occurs to you.

1. _____

_____

2. _____

_____

If you want to reduce someone even further, you can compare him to something not even alive—like two circles. For instance, in *Adam Bede* George Eliot pulled way back from one man and described him as a geometric figure. Mr. Casson struck her as two balls of flesh: a tiny round head on top of a huge belly—a moon, and a giant earth. "On a front view he appeared to consist principally of two spheres, bearing about the same relation to each other as the earth and the moon: that is to say, the lower sphere might be said, at a rough guess, to be thirteen times larger than the upper, which naturally performed the function of a mere satellite and tributary."

EXERCISE

Think, now, of someone who has a lot of contradictions: perhaps a hero or heroine in a movie or in politics. To organize the different ideas you have of that person, you might compare his or her mind to something large and living. Is it a well-trimmed garden, or perhaps an ocean? A forest? A desert? Using concrete terms, describe that "place" in abundant detail.

_____

_____

_____

_____

_____

The most telling image you can use to organize your description is a real one—something you have observed the person doing. If you can quote the person directly, we will be more likely to believe you than if you just pass judgment in vague terms. If you can describe a real scene in which they act this way, we'll believe you more. If you can show that the person acts this way over and over, our conviction will be that much more solid.

H.L. Mencken, the writer, disliked the politician William Jennings Bryan, and looked for some picture that would show why. He fastened on the fact that during his last days of life, Bryan stayed in a country town, swatting flies. How satisfying for Mencken to find this message. Mencken, in fact, called it "peculiarly fitting," because it fits his own bias against Bryan.

> There was something peculiarly fitting in the fact that his last days were spent in a one-horse Tennessee village, beating off the flies and gnats, and that death found him there. The man felt at home in such simple and Christian scenes. He liked people who sweated freely, and were not debauched by the refinements of the toilet. Making his progress up and down the Main Street of little Dayton, Tennessee, surrounded by gaping primates from the upland valleys of the Cumberland Range, his coat laid aside, his bare arms and hairy chest shining damply, his bald head sprinkled with dust—so accoutred and on display, he was obviously happy. [*A Mencken Chrestomathy.*]

Images taken from real observations sound objective, even while you damn a person with his own words. Often such images contain a kernel of argument. For most descriptions of people do serve some larger point—the main theme of a speech, say, or the fundamental idea of a report. William Burroughs calls addiction a form of death, then proves it by accurately reporting his own experiences:

> I lived in one room in the Native Quarter of Tangier. I had not taken a bath in a year nor changed my clothes nor removed them except to stick a needle every hour in the fibrous grey wooden flesh of terminal addiction. I never cleaned or dusted the room. Empty ampule boxes and garbage piled to the ceiling. Light and water long since turned off for non-payment. I did absolutely nothing. I could look at the end of my shoe for eight hours. I was only roused to action when the hourglass of junk ran out. If a friend came to visit—and they rarely did since who or what was left to visit—I sat there not caring that he had entered my field of vision—a grey screen always blanker and fainter—and not caring when he walked out of it. If he had died on the spot I would have sat there looking at my shoe waiting to go through his pockets. Wouldn't you? I never had enough junk—no one ever does. [*Naked Lunch.*]

Take notes on what the person says and does. Not the gist of it: the exact words, the exact gestures. (If you merely sum up what he says, your summary will sound like you. But each person talks in his own way.) Try to snare the unique sound, the peculiar rhythm, the revealing stance. Think like a spy, or Sherlock Holmes.

The real convinces; the abstract merely impresses us. And when you have a larger point to make, your description needs lavish concrete detail to be persuasive.

Even more interesting is writing in which your attitude toward the person slowly changes, deepens. If you organize your material that way, you record a superficial sketch first; then develop a more sensitive portrait; then probe even deeper, for profound analysis. I call this active: for our view of the person changes fairly rapidly, and keeps us busy, trying to put together the different perspectives.

An active description, then, provides us with new insight—possibly even a reversal of what we thought before—every few paragraphs. For instance, you could start by appearing balanced, listing your own high standards, then the person's abject failures, and his pathetic defense of those failures. So far, you have damned the person while seeming objective. But if you want to seem sympathetic and wise as well, you could proceed to say that these facts suggest that the person has some inner conflict—and you could pull out something he said, quoting him exactly, as proof. Having gone deeper into the causes of his behavior now, you produce a different sense of him. If you want to go farther, you might hint at root causes in his background—again quoting him, or someone who is an expert. In this way, we follow you as you delve deeper and deeper.

EXERCISE

Write down three of your earliest childhood memories of your mother, in a few sentences. Be concrete: what did you see, feel, hear?

1. _____

_____

2. _____

_____

3. _____

_____

Now, what general conclusion could you come to about those three incidents?

_____

_____

To probe deeper, what do you know about your mother's own childhood that might throw light on the way she acted toward you when you were young?

_____

_____

_____

What further conclusions, then, might you draw about her relationship with you? _____

_____

We stray from pure abstract reasoning into a discussion of personalities whenever we evaluate someone for a job, reminisce about our past, recommend someone for a promotion, weigh evidence to decide who is to blame, and who is to be praised. We reveal our own standards and prejudices in doing this. Often that interests a reader more than our conclusion: here is a chance for the reader to see how well we judge, how sympathetic we are, how angry, how much care we take with evidence. In writing about real people, our own personality shows.

How to discuss other people:
- Show glimpses: a face, a workspace, a way of dressing.
- Organize your information around a basic image.
- Use a real incident to sum up your feelings about someone.
- Decide on a larger point, and introduce the person as an example.
- Be active: take us step by step deeper into the person's mind and background.
- Quote the person directly. Avoid summaries.
- Describe the person's actions accurately.

VIVID DESCRIPTIONS

Roebuck Ramsden is in his study, opening the morning's letters. The study, handsomely and solidly furnished, proclaims the man of means. Not a speck of dust is visible: it is clear that there are at least two housemaids and a parlormaid downstairs, and a housekeeper upstairs who does not let them spare elbow-grease. Even the top of Roebuck's head is polished: on a sunshiny day he could heliograph his orders to distant camps by merely nodding. In no other respect, however, does he suggest the military man. It is in active civil life that men get his broad air of importance, his dignified expectation of deference, his determinate mouth disarmed and refined since the hour of his success by the withdrawal of opposition and the concession of comfort and precedence and power. He is more than a highly respectable man: he is marked out as a president of highly respectable men, a chairman among directors, an alderman among councillors, a mayor among aldermen. Four tufts of iron-grey hair, which will soon be as white as isinglass, and are in other respects not at all unlike it, grow in two symmetrical pairs above his ears and at the angles of his spreading jaws. He wears a black frock coat, a white waistcoat (it is bright spring weather) and trousers, neither black nor perceptibly blue, of one of those indefinitely mixed hues which the modern clothier has produced to harmonize with the religions of respectable men. He has not been out of doors yet today; so he still wears his slippers, his boots being ready for him on the hearthrug. Surmising that he has no valet, and seeing that he has no secretary with a shorthand notebook and a typewriter, one meditates on how little our great burgess domesticity has been disturbed by new fashions and methods, or by the enterprise of the railway and hotel companies which sell you a Saturday to Monday of life at Folkestone as a real gentleman for two guineas, first class fares both ways included. [George Bernard Shaw, *Man and Superman.*]

T URKEY was a short, pursey Englishman of about my own age, that is, somewhere not far from sixty. In the morning, one might say, his face was a fine florid hue, but after twelve o'clock, meridian—his dinner hour—it blazed like a grate full of Christmas coals; and continued blazing—but, as it were, with a gradual wane—till 6 o'clock P.M. or thereabouts, after which I saw no more of the proprietor of the face, which, gaining its meridian with the sun, seemed to set with it, to rise, culminate, and decline the following day, with the like regularity and undiminished glory. [Herman Melville, *Bartleby the Scrivener.*]

W HEN the young woman—the mother of this child—stood fully revealed before the crowd, it seemed to be her first impulse to clasp the infant closely to her bosom; not so much by an impulse of motherly affection, as that she might thereby conceal a certain token, which was wrought or fastened into her dress. In a moment, however, wisely judging that one token of her shame would but poorly serve to hide another, she took the baby on her arm, and, with a burning blush, and yet a haughty smile, and a glance that would not be abashed, looked around at her townspeople and neighbors. On the breast of her gown, in fine red cloth, surrounded with an elaborate embroidery and fantastic flourishes of gold-thread, appeared the letter A. It was so artistically done, and with so much fertility and gorgeous luxuriance of fancy, that it had all the effect of a last and fitting decoration to the apparel which she wore; and which was of a splendor in accordance with the taste of the age, but greatly beyond what was allowed by the sumptuary regulations of the colony.

The young woman was tall, with a figure of perfect elegance on a large scale. She had dark and abundant hair, so glossy that it threw off the sunshine with a gleam, and a face which, besides being beautiful from regularity of feature and richness of complexion, had the impressiveness belonging to a marked brow and deep black eyes. [Nathaniel Hawthorne, *The Scarlet Letter.*]

4th DAY

Asking Questions

You have nothing to say. Fine. That's normal.

You may have a very vague topic, but you feel empty. Angry, perhaps. Frustrated at the idea of filling up pages with words. Stupid, too, for coming up blank.

If you indulge these feelings for an hour, you can give yourself pains in your belly, back, and head. So I suggest getting around the problem in the following ways.

First, discharge the rage. Part of you—not all, but a strong, unconscious part—does not want to write this report. Think who you're writing it for—in reality, and then, more important, in your imagination. Is anyone else forcing you to write it? Got the names? OK, tell them to leave you alone. You can even cuss them out, under your breath.

Feel better? Now for Step Two. You will be glad to know this does not involve real writing. This step is just preparation. Note-taking. Sketching out ideas. Notice we are postponing doing the actual writing. (Most people force themselves to write before they're ready. Then they criticize themselves word for word, and stop in a funk.) Instead, we are going to whittle your topic down to a manageable idea.

A topic is a word; an idea is a sentence. A topic might be "Love" or "Corporate Earnings," or "Our New Plan." But these subjects seem so vague that you can hardly tell where to begin. What you need is an idea: something to say ABOUT the topic. To get a sense of the difference between a *topic* and an *idea,* try this exercise.

TURNING TOPICS INTO IDEAS

Under the column *Topic* put a food you like or dislike, and then, to the right, under *Idea,* say something about it, something that matters to you.

    Topic   *Idea*

_____   _____

                               _____

_____   _____

_____

_____   _____

_____

_____   _____

Now that you can taste the difference between a general topic and an idea about it, you can see how having a point to make generates other material to talk about. You think oatmeal is mushy? Prove it. That requires you to talk about water, and maybe cream, and cooking, and personal tastes in mushiness.

For this reason, start off by scribbling down your first impression of the topic, in a simple declarative sentence. Not "What should we do about corporate earnings?" But "We should do X about corporate earnings." Not questions, answers. Not a topic, a point.

At this stage, look into your feelings. After all, you're convinced you don't *know* anything about the topic. So go after your reactions. Risk being simple-minded.

This will not be your main point when you actually sit down to write. But it may be close. It may tilt in that direction. Right now, you need a signpost. And your personal bias can tip you to the ideas you care enough about to pursue.

FIRST IMPRESSIONS

Fill in the blanks on the left with places you've visited, neighborhoods, countries, streets, or blocks. Then sum up your first impression on the right.

My first impression of . . .

_____   _____

_____   _____

_____   _____

_____   _____

_____   _____

Whatever ideas you come up with in this free-wheeling will serve as a rough guide, a hypothesis to be tested.

Now for Step Three. In Step Three we ask ourselves dozens of questions about the topic, trying to bring back to mind what we already know, or might look up. We are making loose notes here.

The questions grow out of the ones we commonly ask about anything. They suggest different ways of thinking about anything that interests. They come out of some 2500 years of orators with nothing to say.

Not all of these questions will apply all the time. Some are more appropriate than others to your original topic and idea.

In asking them, look for answers that might help you prove your first impression correct. If after a while you notice that you were wrong, good; revise your main idea. Then see if the other answers support the new one. By asking questions, you bring out material that will strengthen—or force you to refine—your main point.

Here are some basic questions to probe your subject.

- What is it? (What class does it fall into? Is there doubt about that? Does it fall into any other species or category, too?)
- What are its parts? (What parts are needed for it to retain its identity? Which ones are mere decoration or local color? How do these parts fit together, work together? Which function better, which worse?)
- What other thing is it like? How does it compare, exactly? (Also, are you in fact comparing subjects that belong to the same class, or are you comparing oranges with the government? The first is a fair comparison, the second only a juicy analogy.)
- What is it unlike? (Compare it with other subjects in its class; then with subjects far afield. Try, in the process, to pin down what is unique about your own subject.)
- What causes it? (And is that the only cause? Which causes are sufficient to make it happen? Do these things always cause it? What else *could* cause it?)
- What effects does it have? (Are they due only to your subject? Does anything else produce that effect? How wide-ranging are the effects? How serious?)
- Is there anything which is the complete opposite? Opposite in certain areas?
- Is your subject a means to some end? If so, what? How does it bring about that end?
- Is your subject an end toward which other things lead? If so, what kind of result is it?
- Is your subject scarce or abundant? And is it worth more because of that?
- Is your subject popular or unpopular? And what does that prove about it?
- Do people argue about your subject? In what areas? Why?

The effort here is to turn up material, not necessarily to answer every question. Follow doubts. For instance, if you spot some uncertainty, pursue it. Ask more questions about that. If some answer seems pious, but not really true for you, press on until you find a more honest and accurate answer. As you might imagine, such notes wander all over several pages. Let them. You are not ready to organize.

In medieval courts, lawyers came prepared with three main questions: "An sit, quid sit, quale sit?" Roughly translated, the lawyer wanted to know "Whether it happened; then, if it did happen, what exactly happened; then, if it is proved the crime occurred, what kind was it?"

During this process, examples will come to mind. Some may seem extraneous.

Put them down anyway. Some seem important, though you cannot say why: jot down the names, or some key facts. You can figure out the application later.

Given enough raw material, your mind will make sense of it. And in fact, by putting down your first impressions, you have already seen it do so. Constantly refer back to that idea to see if you are proving it, disproving it, or wandering into new areas. (That's OK, but if you find them interesting you may have to open up your main idea to include them.)

Pick an event you like to think about, or a general process, or perhaps a pet solution to some big problem. What's your theory? Where do you stand? (Don't think too much. Just say the first thing that comes to mind.) Now you have a sentence saying what you think about the topic—not just saying, "In this paper I will discuss the process of growing tobacco," but explaining that "I will prove that hanging gauze over tobacco helps it grow." So you can proceed to define your terms, find its parts, spell out its relationship with other subjects—and, throughout, hone your main idea.

AN ACTIVE EXERCISE

Pick as a topic some event or process.

What is your topic? _____

What do you have to say about it, at first? _____

_____

Now in this activity, what are the key things that happen? _____

_____

What is the sequence? _____

_____

Who does what, when, to whom, and why? _____

_____

_____

_____

What type of activity would you classify this as? _____

_____

What are its stages? _____

_____

What other activities is it like? _____

_____

Unlike? _____

What are the causes? _____

_____

Results? _____

_____

_____

What value does this activity have? _____

_____

Is this activity inevitable? _____

Could this activity be changed? How? _____

_____

_____

Is this activity rare? _____

Popular? _____

What areas of controversy surround this activity? _____

_____

_____

You could probably write a chapter in answer to each question, and that is why you need to start with an idea—not just a topic. A topic seems infinite. From almost any topic, you can range into everything it touches or suggests. You wander without beginning or end, and you have no purpose, except to ramble on.

But an idea—a sentence—limits your work. If you can state your idea in one straightforward sentence, you have something to prove. That means you don't have to explore everything about the topic; you can ignore what seems irrelevant. In addition, you have something to chase: evidence to prove your point.

By asking questions—then asking questions about the answers—you can open up whole areas of evidence. In the next chapter, we will go into some ways of organizing that material when you write. But for the moment think of the pleasure of taking random notes. Some seem trivial. Others, important. Some show you how much you don't know; others how much you do. And a few suggest cracks in the conventional explanation—flaws in the party line. By driving a wedge into these fissures, you open up a chance to see the whole subject from a new angle.

So, when you feel stumped, start out by blowing off your anger at having to write at all, then jot down your first impression of the subject, and chip away at that idea by asking, asking, asking.

SOME EXAMPLES

WHAT would men have? Do they think those they employ and deal with are saints? Do they not think they will have their own ends, and be truer to themselves than to them? Therefore there is no better way to moderate suspicions, than to count such suspicions as true, and yet to bridle them as false. [Francis Bacon, "Of Suspicion."]

T HIS is one of the new relationships in a transient society for which there is no word or phrase in common use. Marian and I were not friends, because friendship grows out of mutual concerns and out of being together at many times in many places. We were not lovers, because there was little or no continuity of desire. We were not completely casual libertines, dissolute and uncontrolled. Each of us had fed a great many bits into our personal computers, at breakneck speed. Is he-she physically attractive to me? Is he-she clean and healthy? Will he-she be circumspect and private about it? Is he-she seeking some kind of angle or advantage I don't know about? Is he-she likely to be kinky in some kind of vulgar, unpleasant or even alarming way? Could he-she be hunting some kind of long-range emotional security and personal involvement I can't afford? Are there so many shadow areas in the computer response to the questions that the anticipated pleasure is not worth the unknown risk? [John D. MacDonald, *The Turquoise Lament.*]

5th DAY

Organizing Your Notes

Now to organize those rough notes. You have an idea, and you have some evidence—some strong, some silly—to back it up. How are you going to proceed?

"Outline!" says Miss Metcalf, the high-school teacher. Yes, outline. But most of us have felt the hopelessness of filling out a form that looks like this:

Main Point
    1. First main proof
        a. subordinate evidence
        b. subordinate evidence
        c. subordinate evidence
    2. Second main proof
        a. subordinate evidence
        b. subordinate evidence
        c. subordinate evidence

That's a reasonable outline. But few people could fill it out right off. A detailed outline should form the last step, not the first, when you get down to organizing.

Instead of locking yourself into an outline, and stolidly writing it out, pause for a moment to think about the people you are writing for. What are they like? What matters most to them? To you? What tone of voice do you want to approach them with?

Tone comes from the strategy you choose when you start talking. Do you want to persuade the reader, primarily, through intellectual argument? Or do you want to move the reader's emotions? Or are you going to stay on a high plateau, and urge the reader to respond to an ethical appeal? Each strategy (intellectual, emotional, ethical) means a different choice of evidence.

If you want to move people by appealing to their conscience, you will have to show that you can pass inspection yourself. Machiavelli, for instance, advised his prince to *look* virtuous in order to succeed in crime.

But how can you boast of your own good will, generosity, compassion, uprightness, wit, and wisdom? How prove you are just? How indeed? If you sense you lack some traces of moral perfection, you may want to back off from a purely ethical argument, for a moment of snappishness can ruin your carefully worked-up image. And a flare of anger, or a joke that is off-color, can stain your saintly costume.

Actually, most of what people think will be an appeal to conscience seems to end up being a cry of rage or sorrow. In effect, the writer has shifted from abstract grounds of right and wrong to the turf of the novelist and stump speaker.

ETHICAL EXERCISE

In the general area of transportation (bus, car, walking), take a firm, ethical position for or against something that stops traffic.

Who is your audience? ———————————————————————

What proves your virtue on this topic? ——————————————

————————————————————————————————————

What do you condemn, morally? ————————————————————

————————————————————————————————————

————————————————————————————————————

What emotional scene would help you persuade your audience you are right?

————————————————————————————————————

————————————————————————————————————

————————————————————————————————————

What do people feel emotional about? We can guess from the news. Sex and violence, Mom and Dad. God and food, to judge from what books sell the most. Cash, and a quiet night.

You might ask yourself if you are going to probe any of these things directly—describing scenes in which they play a key role, encouraging the reader to think about them, explaining them, or helping the reader find satisfaction with them. If so, you may want to organize your material on an emotional staircase, leading from the least moving to the most upsetting material.

If you are not exploring material that is obviously emotional, you may still want to arouse emotions. First, figure out what feelings you harbor for the subject. Are they all nostalgic? Do you also feel some fear? Anger? The more you know your own reactions, the easier it will be for you to focus on the events that evoke these feelings in you, and probably in your audience too.

In this strategy, you do not tell the reader you are going to make him angry. You make him angry. How? By selecting the very details—the concrete evidence—that disturb you most. Put them in the order that rattles you. If you do, he may get mad too. Consider Shirley Chisholm's addition:

> There are 435 members of the House of Representatives and 417 are white
> males. Ten of the others are women, and nine are black. I belong to both of
> these minorities, which makes it add up right. That makes me a celebrity, a

kind of side-show attraction. I was the first American citizen to be elected to Congress in spite of the double drawbacks of being female and having skin darkened by melanin.

When you put it that way, it sounds like a foolish reason for fame. In a just and free society it would be foolish. That I am a national figure because I was the first person in 192 years to be at once a congressman, black, and a woman proves, I would think, that our society is not yet either just or free. [*Unbought and Unbossed.*]

OUTBURST

Think of the way you commonly travel around town, and concentrate on a particular hassle. Now, what should be done about it? _____

_____

Who would you tell about this? _____

_____

What emotions do you feel when you meet this problem? _____

_____

What specific things arouse the emotions? (Think of what you see, feel, touch, smell, hear.) _____

_____

_____

_____

But, you say, what if I am writing something purely logical? Me, I doubt it.

Even the most intellectual writing harbors some emotion under the surface. Beneath Shirley Chisholm's arithmetic boils real anger. One essayist lashes out at other scholars who have let down the high standards of the profession: what is this but pique and anger? Another expert points out the flaws in the macroeconomic theories of his fellow expert; underneath, he is also saying, look at me, I'm better. The more you try to hide such feelings, the more gobbledygook you write to cover them up.

An intellectual dissecting a weak argument resembles a fencing master slashing a student's shirt apart. Beautiful, but often nasty.

Look for the parts in your story or essay that light up for you. Focus on what disturbs you. What puzzles you? What seems wrong? Follow your emotions to discover intellectual errors, to clear up ethical confusion, and you will find which parts of your evidence will work most strongly on your reader.

When you begin to organize your notes, consider the emotional possibilities first. Some items in your notes matter more, carry a larger emotional charge. Those belong in important positions: very early in your piece, or, say, two-thirds of the way through, at a climax. Other items are necessary background: put them before whatever they prepare. Still other items necessarily come later in the discussion: they are last in time, or farthest away in space, or less significant to the main point.

So far you have been casting a rough order: what goes before, what seems most important, what seems minor. Time for a fresh sheet of paper—your first outline.

At the top: your main idea, in a sentence.

Under that, the main proofs, in big letters, with plenty of white space around them.

Then some of the minor proofs, in approximate order.

That gives you the basic shape of what you are going to write: the main landmarks.

Now it's time to look into each of those main proofs in detail. For each one you may have to run through another battery of questions. You may have to reach out to books and computer printouts for research. You may decide to interview someone for first-hand reactions. But now you know how that information is supposed to fit into your overall argument. So you can home in on it faster. You can skip the data that do not help. You can insist that the expert you talk to really tells you the answers you need.

Only after you've gone through that process—for a few hours or weeks, depending on the scale of your project—can you finally sit down and fill out Miss Metcalf's outline.

Meanwhile, you will probably find you have reworded your main argument. From note taking, you may have suspected that your idea was a little vague, or else obvious. If so, adjust it to apply to the material you've turned up; it should sum up what you have found.

Also, does your main idea say something new? Does it in some way challenge conventional theory? If not, why write it? Look through your material, think about the areas of doubt and controversy; if possible, take a position there. Be bold: follow your own intuitive reactions.

You will make your job easier if you make sure your main idea is only one idea. People often come up with double-barrel thoughts that require two sets of proof, rather than just one. A bank officer who writes, "The borrower has substantial net worth, and therefore can be trusted to complete construction on schedule," in effect promises to prove, first, that the borrower has a lot of money and second, that more money will somehow help the borrower finish construction on time. If you notice you have forced yourself to demonstrate two or more points, rethink and condense.

FOOT EXERCISE

Take a firm position on your feet. Are they terrific?

I think my feet are _____
Now jot down in a word or two the things you would use to prove that:

A. _____

B. _____

C. _____

D. _____

E. _____

Put a big star by the proof that seems to have the biggest impact. Put a two by the second-best proof. Turn these two ideas into sentences designed to prove your main point:

1. _____

_____

2. _____

_____

Now recast your main idea so that it better expresses the material you've kicked up:

_____

Having revised your thesis, you may want to switch around the order of proofs. You may have discovered new ones, or dropped a few that turned out to be embarrassing or trivial. If you do not feel your proofs fall into a logical or natural order, you might sort them into one of these common patterns:
1. The process: you go step by step, in time.
2. The map: you go step by step, in a place.
3. The problem—and solution: you set up a puzzling problem at the beginning, then suggest a solution—and prove that yours works.
4. Classifying: you break up a larger subject into smaller classes, for discussion.
5. Point and proofs: you simply state your point, and line up your proofs.

Once you have an almost perfect outline, critique it again. You might consider putting the best proof last, and the second-best proof first, if you care most about making a strong finale. Or you might feel that clarity matters more, in which case you might move from the first to the last item, from smallest to biggest, from easy-to-grasp to complex and difficult-to-understand ideas. In brief, ask: is there a real reason for my order?

As you move into your final outline—the one you will actually work from as you write—keep turning any mere topic into full sentences. This will keep you from postponing thinking about how they actually support your point.

And think of each subsection as proof. Each one provides a key clarifying detail—and as you scan your outline, you should have a firm idea of how each one adds to your over-all argument. (A list of topics stays limp in a row; a chain of arguments develops intensity as you read; proofs build.)

You see, what actually goes on is an ebb and flow. You get a rough outline, you break it down, you build up a new one, you explore each part of that, you fix your main argument, you reorder your proofs, you make your own thoughts clear to yourself.

Throughout, make the effort to get straight what you personally think. (Otherwise, this work ends up being only an exercise in taking notes or shuffling paper.) Done with an eye on your own real reactions, this process can give your writing coherence, and emotional force.

So . . .

- Do not rush into an outline.
- Do not fix on one main idea and never change it.
  In fact . . .
  - if you don't know where to start
  - if you are not sure of what you want to say
  - if you are not even sure what to look up
  - if you aren't sure of your own emotional stand . . .
  SLOW DOWN.

In brief, to find a coherent, strong theme, follow these suggestions as you scratch preliminary notes:

- Decide whether your approach will be mainly ethical, emotional, or intellectual.
- Recognize your own gut reactions, and use them to form your main idea.
- Figure out a tentative argument, and aim to prove it.
- Test and refine your main idea, by asking:
  —Is it a simple sentence?
  —Is it clear?
  —Does it make one point, not two or three?
  —Is it specific?
  —Does it go beyond the obvious?
  Test your rough outline by asking:
  —What areas do I need to study more before writing?
  —Does the evidence really prove the point?
  —Is there a real reason for this order?
  Set up—and revise—a continuously growing outline.

EXAMPLES

Here are examples of a strongly felt main point, with a quick outline of the author's proofs:

THE Big Bull Market was dead. Billions of dollars' worth of profits and paper profits had disappeared. The grocer, the window-cleaner, and the seamstress had lost their capital. In every town there were families which had suddenly dropped from showy affluence into debt. Investors who had dreamed of retiring to live on their fortunes now found themselves back once more at the very beginning of the long road to riches. Day by day the newspapers printed the grim reports of suicides. [Frederick Lewis Allen, *Only Yesterday.*]

IF you find ants crawling over your plants, look for other troubles. The ants themselves do no harm except that they carry the young of mealybugs, aphids, and scale insects from place to place.

Ants are there in search of food, and the food they seek is the sweet, sticky secretion known as honeydew, which is given off by scale insects, whiteflies, aphids, and mealybugs. Therefore, if ants are present, look carefully for one or more of these pests. Remove these and the ants will cease visiting your plants. [T.H. Everett, *How to Grow Beautiful House Plants.*]

THE history of the present King of Great Britain in a history of repeated injuries and usurpations, all having in direct object the establishment of an absolute tyranny over these states. To prove this, let facts be submitted to a candid world.

He has refused his assent to laws the most wholesome and necessary for the public good.

He has forbidden his governors to pass laws of immediate and pressing importance, unless suspended in their operation till his assent should be obtained; and when so suspended, he has utterly neglected to attend to them.

He has refused to pass other laws for the accommodation of large districts of people, unless those people would relinquish the right of representation in the legislature; a right inestimable to them and formidable to tyrants only.

He has called together legislative bodies at places unusual, uncomfortable, and distant from the depository of their public records, for the sole purpose of fatiguing them into compliance with his measures.

He has dissolved Representative Houses repeatedly, for opposing, with manly firmness, his invasions on the rights of the People.

He has refused for a long time, after such dissolutions, to cause others to be elected; whereby the Legislative Powers, incapable of annihilation, have returned to the people at large for their exercise; the state remaining in the mean time exposed to all the dangers of invasion from without, and convulsions within.

He has endeavored to prevent the population of these states; for that purpose obstructing the Laws of Naturalization of foreigners; refusing to pass others to encourage their migrations hither, and raising the conditions of new appropriations of lands.

He has obstructed the administration of justice, by refusing his assent to laws for establishing judiciary powers.

He has made judges dependent on his will alone, for the tenure of their offices, and the amount and payment of their salaries.

He has erected a multitude of new offices, and sent hither swarms of officers to harass our people, and eat out their substance.

He has kept among us, in times of peace, standing armies, without the consent of our legislatures.

He has affected to render the military independent of and superior to the civil power. [Declaration of Independence.]

6th DAY

Drawing Parallels

When someone asked the writer Anatole France what he thought were the three most important qualities of French style, he said, "First of all, clarity; then, more clarity; and finally, clarity."

If you want people to remember your point, repeat it simply. Emphasize the fact that you are repeating yourself by using the same word, or the same sound, or the same grammatical construction. When we see the same format over and over, we expect the contents to be the same. Same bottle, same wine, we think.

For instance, when Caesar swept into Rome, someone asked him how he had taken over the city, despite the protests of the Senate, the objections of upper-class politicians, and the opposition of some segments of the army. He said, *"Veni, vidi, vici"*—"I came, I saw, I conquered."

That clipped summary is easy to recall. Caesar repeats sounds (the *v* and the *i*), rhythms (each Latin word has two syllables), and grammatical form (first person, past tense). He sums up his attitude as well—the three words sound powerful, tight-lipped, effective, like a commander. That was the impression he wanted to make—that for him conquering was no harder than seeing or traveling. Setting himself off from the talky, indecisive Senate, he beat the politicians in part because of his taut, even brutal style.

EXERCISE

Using the same sound to begin each word in a list, describe some familiar experiences:

On TV I see _____ (*D*'s)

When I eat junk food, I taste _____ (*P*'s)

Home means mmm ... _____ (*M*'s)

Make two opposites sound like one. Choose two words that have opposite meanings, but begin with the same sounds.

S _____ is s _____ .

H _____ is h _____ .

P _____ is p _____ .

When we talk, we often use parallelism, without being aware of it. We may use it to pound in our point; we use it to show that several ideas are similar; and we use it to suggest that things are similar even if they are not. Diane Narek, a scientist, recalls the first moon landing: "On July 22, 1969, several of my friends and I were watching the astronauts land on the moon. We watched and asked the same question, 'Why aren't there any women astronauts on the moon?' 'Why aren't there any women technicians?' 'How are we kept from these fields?' "

The same anger seems to fire each question. And we sense that, in part, because each follows a similar format (first a *why* or *how;* then the verb *are;* then a negative idea; then the word *women,* for themselves; then another referring to their field, science). In this way, Narek suggests that all three questions do spring from the same reaction.

In public meetings, talking in parallel structure can help an audience see a similar pattern, feel a similar emotion, in a whole series of different situations. In 1965, for instance, during a protest march from Selma to Montgomery, Alabama, Martin Luther King, Jr., said: "We are moving to the land of freedom. Let us march to the realization of the American dream. Let us march on segregated housing. Let us march on segregated schools. Let us march on poverty. Let us march on ballot boxes, march on ballot boxes until race baiters disappear from the political arena, until the Wallaces of our nation tremble away in silence."

The audience loved this. They fell into his rhythm. They came to expect his phrase, "Let us march." They began to say it themselves, so that it became their own.

EXERCISE

First, imagine moving through your own neighborhood, from the farthest corner, through the middle, and back to your front door. First place you see: _____

Next: _____

Next: _____

Next: _____

Next: _____

Next: _____

And nearest to your door: _____

Now, using those places in that order, talk about repairing or tearing down, or fighting in your neighborhood. Imagine you are talking to a large group of friends and neighbors. Start each sentence with the same phrase, as King did.

_____

_____

_____

_____

Parallelism can help you overcome distinctions your audience usually makes. St. Basil heard his followers distinguish between rich men and poor men, but he saw them both as human. And he saw that men only need a certain amount to live on, and that the rich could live on less, so he imagined that if we each took only what we really need from some general pot, then we would all be equally well off: "If everyone would take only according to his needs, and would leave the surplus to the needy, no one would be rich, no one poor, no one miserable."

To suggest how each class would lose its distinctiveness, he treats each the same way (no one would be ... no one ... no one). He makes them look alike, to argue that they can in fact be made to _be_ alike.

EXERCISE

Think of some people's excuses for higher prices or shoddy work. People think each excuse is unique, but you may be forgiven for feeling they are all somehow the same—just excuses. Make up a list of them, beginning with the same phrase, showing you think they're all equal—equally bad. (They say ... they say ... they say.)

_____

_____

_____

_____

Since parallel form suggests that everything in the series is the same, some writers use it to demonstrate that, really, each item is different.

Lester Markel of _The New York Times_, for instance, noticed that his reporters could not tell the difference between hard news, background information, and their own opinion. This mush of fact, feeling, and irrelevant data came out in the papers as if it were all true. So Markel decided to set things straight by distinguishing between three things usually blurred together:

"What you see is news, what you know is background, what you feel is opinion."

Parallelism helps us remember another important distinction. Before his inaugural, John F. Kennedy and his speech writers knew that most people who came to call wanted something for themselves, but talked as if it would be good for the country. Fed up with this, he turned the terms around, using parallelism to make his phrases easy to recall:

"Ask not what your country can do for you: ask what you can do for your country."

In the simplest way, repeating an idea over and over drives it home. Repeating the point makes people think about it, now in one way, now in another, until they cannot escape feeling it, tasting it, recalling their own experience of it. Here's a paragraph by Hemingway.

> You got very hungry when you did not eat enough in Paris because all the bakery shops had such good things in the windows and people ate outside at tables on the sidewalk so that you saw and smelled the food. When you had given up journalism and were writing nothing that anyone in America would buy, explaining at home that you were lunching out with someone, the best place to go was the Luxembourg gardens where you saw and smelled nothing to eat all the way from the Place de l'Observatoire to the rue de Vaugirard. There you could always go into the Luxembourg museum and all the paintings were sharpened and clearer and more beautiful if you were belly-empty, hollow-hungry. I learned to understand Cézanne much better and to see truly how he made landscapes when I was hungry. I used to wonder if he were hungry too when he painted; but I thought possibly it was only that he had forgotten to eat. It was one of those unsound but illuminating thoughts you have when you have been sleepless or hungry. Later I thought Cézanne was probably hungry in a different way. [*A Moveable Feast.*]

EXERCISE

Think of some strong feeling you've had over a long time, in a number of places, then write a paragraph bringing in the same word over and over the way Hemingway does.

Word you will repeat: ———————————————

———————————————————————————————————

———————————————————————————————————

———————————————————————————————————

———————————————————————————————————

———————————————————————————————————

———————————————————————————————————

To sum up: parallelism means repeating your form. How?
  — Repeating the same word over and over.
  — Using the same grammatical construction over and over.
  — Beginning each phrase with the same word.
  — Beginning each sentence with the same word.
  — Echoing the same vowel sounds or consonants.
And putting words into parallel form can help you to:
  — Pound in your main point.
  — Make people remember it.

— Show that you intend to do the same thing in different areas or situations.
— Make a number of different ideas seem similar.
— Distinguish between ideas most people think are the same.

EXAMPLES OF PARALLELISM

IF nominated, I will not accept; if elected, I will not serve. [William Tecumseh Sherman.]

HE lays himself down upon her without previous toying, he does not kiss her, nor twine himself round her; he does not bite her, nor suck her lips, nor tickle her.

He gets upon her before she has begun to long for pleasure, and then he introduces with infinite trouble a member soft and nerveless. Scarcely has he commenced when he is already done for; he makes one or two movements, and then sinks upon the woman's breast to spend his sperm; and that is the most he can do. This done, he withdraws his affair, and makes all haste to get down again from her.

Such a man—as was said by a writer—is quick in ejaculation and slow as to erection; after the trembling, which follows the ejaculation of the seed, his chest is heavy and his sides ache.

Qualities like these are no recommendation with women. [Shaykh Nefsawi, *The Perfumed Garden,* trans. Sir Richard Burton.]

THERE are young men who are dead this week who should be alive, and it would be a horrible thing no matter who they were. But of course they were Jews; the reason that they are dead is because they were Jews, and that is why on this night there are so many of us starting to realize for the first time what that means.

It is not supposed to be very strong in us, for we cannot remember. We grew up laughing at the solemn old Jewish phrases that sounded so mournful and outmoded and out of date in the second half of the twentieth century. Ancient, outmoded phrases from the temples, phrases like "Let my people go." Phrases that we chose to let mean nothing, because it is not supposed to be very strong in us. [Bob Greene, *Johnny Deadline, Reporter.*]

7th DAY

Sharpening a Contrast

Draw sharp contrasts to silhouette your own views. You can cast your opponent down into darkness, you can highlight your own ideas.

Even before writing, think of opposites that will generate new topics to talk about, by mulling over the ways your particular subject differs from other things. Perhaps it is confused with A. Perhaps it falls into the same general category as B & C. Perhaps it shares one trait in common with D. But your subject probably differs in some important ways from A, B, C, and D. By noting these differences, you may be able to pinpoint the unique qualities of your own subject or idea.

In writing, a gift for sharp distinctions can help you save space. You can reverse an opponent's argument with one phrase rather than with three paragraphs of rambling. You can pin down exactly where you disagree with someone. And in this way you can clarify your own meaning. By showing exactly where you differ from others, you can give depth and color to your own views.

Any strong contrast pivots on a common point. Yes, man is weak, but he thinks, so he can overcome his weakness. Yes, man lacks something, but what he lacks is not strength, but will. The crucial step in evolving a contrast, then, is to figure out not just what subjects are similar, but what areas, what parts, show the sharpest contrast.

For instance, G.K. Chesterton wrote, "There are two equal and eternal ways of looking at this twilight world of ours: we may see it as the twilight of evening, or the twilight of morning; we may think of anything, down to a fallen acorn, as a descendant or as an ancestor."

Chesterton wanted to compare two attitudes, both somewhat sentimental, both glimmering with half-light. In one view, our world is just at the edge of dawn; in the other, at the edge of night. By stressing the common element of an almost eternal twilight, he can make clear the opposing moods of decline and rebirth; and the opposing conceptions of an acorn as beginning, or as end.

Again, we might think that martyrs suffer for their beliefs. But does that mean that their beliefs are right? The answers may differ. One person might say death does prove the martyr's beliefs were correct, but the Austrian writer Arthur Schnitzler felt that: "Martyrdom has always been proof of the intensity, not of the correctness of a belief." In the first part of his sentence, he sets up the common ground (that martyrdom must prove something), then draws the distinction (between two views of what it proves) in the second half.

DEBUNKING

Debunk some popular beliefs about what causes personal suffering as you fill in the blanks in these contrasts. (The common point is *cause*, here.)

Acne is not due to _____; it's due to _____.

_____ does not cause accidents; _____ does.

We break down, not because _____

_____

but because _____.

Sometimes, if we follow differences far enough, we may discover some stark contraries. Edward Corbett, a teacher, explains:

"*Liberty* and *licence* would be an example of difference; *liberty* and *slavery* would be an example of contraries."

Complete opposites, of course, are rare in ordinary life. But two people, alike in blondness, say, might be complete opposites in their view of the meaning of life or power.

"The opposition between the men who have, and the men who are, is immemorial," said the philosopher William James, in *The Varieties of Religious Experience*.

"You shall have joy, or you shall have power, said God; you shall not have both," wrote Ralph Waldo Emerson, in his Civil War journal. Just how he knew what God had said, Emerson doesn't tell us. But the distinction between the two things we might "have" seems total—absolute as one of the commandments: we shall not have both of them at once.

Sometimes an extreme contrast breaks down, upon examination, and we see that it is just the words that are opposites. *Rich* is the opposite of *poor,* but a rich person may actually be a lot like some poor person. Best, then, to make sure you have some real contrast underneath.

We may feel a real original behind Samuel Johnson's careful description of the Reverend Zachariah Mudge: "Though studious, he was popular; though argumentative, he was modest; though inflexible, he was candid; and though metaphysical, yet orthodox."

TWO PEOPLE

Think of two real people you know, as opposite as can be. Then fill out this list to discover the most striking contrasts. For instance, which is stronger? In what respect?

Stronger? _____ Weaker? _____ In what area? _____

Smarter? _____ Dumber? _____ In what area? _____

Graceful? ——————— Klutzy? ——————— In what area? ———————

Louder? ——————— Quieter? ——————— In what area? ———————

Gentle? ——————— Rough? ——————— In what area? ———————

More beautiful? ——— Uglier? ——————— In what area? ———————

Fun? ——————— Unpleasant? ——— In what area? ———————

Healthy? ——————— Unhealthy? ——— In what area? ———————

Now pick the three most revealing contrasts, and sum up the difference between these two people in a few sentences. Remember that you are trying to give someone else a picture of the real difference between the two of them.

———————————————————————————————

———————————————————————————————

———————————————————————————————

REVISING FOR CONTRAST

Remember parallelism? Hear how awkward some contrasts sound when one half comes out skewed or crippled for lack of parallelism. Take this first draft:

> In judging the man as a friend, and as a citizen of England, Essex thought that somehow Sir Francis Bacon lacked a little enthusiasm, at least as a friend; their queen, Queen Elizabeth, thought he was occasionally not too loyal to her, at least as a subject.

If we emphasize the common attitude more, then the contrast becomes more obvious:

> At times Essex thought that Sir Francis Bacon lacked enthusiasm as a friend; Queen Elizabeth thought he lacked loyalty as a subject.

Here is another first draft:

> From a distance, war seems clean, but up close we know that most people find war filthy, sweaty, and chaotic. Here at home we look at lines moving across maps, we don't see half an arm lying on a runway, or a real landscape exploding. Stateside, we watch, but over there, we smell something burning—a pile of bodies, perhaps—and we throw up.

If we cut about half the words, and sharpen the parallel structure, the contrasts emerge:

> From a distance, war seems clean; comforted with the steam of fresh coffee, we look at lines on maps; we see statistics; we watch. But up close, war gets us dirty; we feel a real landscape exploding; lying on the runway, we see half an arm; at the smell of burning bodies, we vomit.

So revise each of the following sentences to make the parallels—and therefore the contrasts—more visible.

1. Disasters shock us—sometimes—into seeing what we've been doing wrong. But sometimes, like when an earthquake happens or a flood comes, disasters just crush us and don't mean anything to us, because we're so overwhelmed, you know.

_____

_____

_____

_____

2. They say experience is a great school—the university of hard-knocks—and I guess so, but experience takes a long time to teach, and if it were a real school, you'd say the course sure took a long time—a lifetime—so when you graduate, you're too old, or worn out, to do much with the lesson.

_____

_____

_____

_____

3. She hates to wash dishes, or sponge up butter on the linoleum, or scoot the toast crumbs into the garbage. He likes a super-neat dish rack, and a smooth table top, and floors that don't stick to your feet. She thinks Mom should clean up after her; he's different, not better, just different. I guess he thinks Mom will be happy if he cleans up. Two people: one house.

_____

_____

_____

_____

_____

When we use only a few words to compare two people in terms of age, rank, and wisdom, say, we can deal with each aspect of the first person (A: 1, 2, 3), then do the same for the second person (B: 1, 2, 3), assuming the reader can match up the contrasting areas. "He was a stupid old politician, and she was a smart young singer."

But when the ground for contrast involves a few sentences, or even a few paragraphs, the reader may not see how the contrasts work, since they appear so far apart. In such cases we may find it easier to organize by topics, contrasting A to B first in terms of age (1: A vs. B), then in terms of rank (2: A vs. B), then in terms of occupation (3: A vs. B). This organization carries out the overall contrast, topic by topic.

TWO PLACES

Think of two very different places you know well—towns, rooms, offices, or streets. First take some notes on the differences.

Place A _____ Place B _____

What you are contrasting: _____

Describe that in A: _____

Describe that in B: _____

What you are contrasting: _____

Describe that in A: _____

Describe that in B: _____

What you are contrasting: _____

Describe that in A: _____

Describe that in B: _____

Now organize these notes into a full paragraph, contrasting the two places. Your first sentence, of course, should sum up the main difference you find. Then proceed topic by topic, being sure you include both places under each topic. (Contrasts are like pairs of shoes; when you drop one, the reader waits to hear the other fall).

Of course, sometimes you'll find that there are twenty counts against a place, and only one thing for it—but that one is important. Here, for instance, is the way William Congreve organizes two contrasting views on love:

> *Fainall:* For a passionate lover, methinks you are a man somewhat too discerning in the failings of your mistress.

> *Mirabell:* And for a discerning man, somewhat too passionate a lover; for I like her with all her faults—nay, like her for her faults. Her follies are so natural, or so artful, that they become her; and those affectations which in another woman would be odious, serve but to make her more agreeable. [*The Way of the World.*]

A paradox includes the wildest opposites within one thing—a skyline, or a person's mental outlook. The nineteenth-century writer, William Hazlitt, liked talking with people indoors, but not outdoors; he felt nature was companion enough on his walks.

"One of the pleasantest things in the world is going a journey," he wrote. "But

I like to go by myself. I can enjoy society in a room; but out of doors, nature is company enough for me. I am then never less alone than when alone."

By repeating the word *alone,* Hazlitt emphasizes that when others might look at him out in the fields, and think him "alone," he does not feel alone, because he receives so much from nature.

We may be forced to use a paradox to sum up situations in which the contrasting elements fight each other at close range, expressing intense emotions. Here are some Hollywood examples:

"Death scenes are dearer than life to the actor."

—Louise Brooks.

"Marilyn Monroe was a professional amateur."

—Laurence Olivier.

"When I'm good I'm very good, but when I'm bad, I'm better."

—Mae West.

"I don't want to achieve immortality through my work. I want to achieve it through not dying."

—Woody Allen.

I VS. ME

Write a paragraph summing up some of the areas in which you are pulled in different directions, for example, liking one thing and its reverse, knowing one thing but thinking the opposite, too, seeing yourself as a blend of contrary impulses. What are your most startling contrasts? You might start with the idea,

"I am a paradox." ———————————————————————————

——————————————————————————————————————

——————————————————————————————————————

——————————————————————————————————————

——————————————————————————————————————

To sum up: in contrasting two things, we need to . . .
  — make clear the topic on which we find them at odds
  — use parallel form, if possible, to sharpen that contrast
  — organize by topics, or subjects, depending on length.
And when should we emphasize a contrast? Whenever we want to . . .
  — show how one thing (or idea, or person) differs from another, or
  — explain the conflicts within a given person, or event, or
  — distinguish our own views from someone else's, or
  — sum up both sides of a paradoxical feeling.

EXAMPLES OF HIGH CONTRAST

CRAFT must have clothes, but truth loves to go naked. [Thomas Fuller.]

PROPERTY is theft. [Pierre Proudhon.]

IF you strike a child, take care that you strike it in anger, even at the risk of maiming it for life. A blow in cold blood neither can nor should be forgiven. [George Bernard Shaw.]

THE man with a toothache thinks everyone happy whose teeth are sound. The poverty-stricken man makes the same mistake about the rich man. [George Bernard Shaw.]

DON JUAN (*to the Devil*): Pooh! Why should I be civil to them or to you? In this Palace of Lies a truth or two will not hurt you. Your friends are all the dullest dogs I know. They are not beautiful: they are only decorated. They are not clean: they are only shaved and starched. They are not dignified: they are only fashionably dressed. They are not educated: they are only college passmen. They are not religious: they are only pew-renters. They are not moral: they are only conventional. They are not virtuous: they are only cowardly. They are not even vicious: they are only "frail." They are not artistic: they are only lascivious. They are not prosperous; they are only rich. They are not loyal, they are only servile; not dutiful, only sheepish; not public spirited, only patriotic; not courageous, only quarrelsome; not determined, only obstinate; not masterful, only domineering; not self-controlled, only obtuse; not self-respecting, only vain; not kind, only sentimental; not social, only gregarious; not considerate, only polite; not intelligent, only opinionated; not progressive, only factious; not imaginative, only superstitious; not just, only vindictive; not generous, only propitiatory; not disciplined, only cowed; and not truthful at all—liars every one of them, to the very backbone of their souls. [George Bernard Shaw, *Man and Superman.*]

8th DAY
Finding More Evidence

Yes, you can always find more evidence. You can read more, scan more video displays, computer print-outs, maps, charts, and graphs. You can go out and talk to experts, people with experience, idle bystanders. You can poll, poke, test, and cast nets.

Why bother? If you pile up a hundred examples in your notes, you will easily pick the half-dozen that make your point best. Sharp research fills pages, challenges your own initial ideas, provides real proof.

Too much random study, though, simply chokes the mind. Focus, then, on your main point: find proof for THAT, and let the other data go.

When you are reading fast, scan for the author's point. How does that tie in with yours? If it is not relevant, skip to the next article or book. If the author discusses your subject pertinently, then his main point is worth copying out for future use. So is his evidence. When you record it, though, do more than mention a name or two. For your own sake, include enough detail so that you can use this evidence later, without going vague at the edges.[1] Here, for instance, we have the result of wide reading aimed at proving that all famous men are eccentric.

> Forgetfulness is one of the characteristics of genius. It is said that Newton once rammed his niece's finger into his pipe; when he left his room to seek for something he usually returned without bringing it. Rouelle generally explained his ideas at great length, and when he had finished, he added: "But this is one of my arcana, which I tell to no one." Sometimes one of his pupils rose and repeated in his ear what he had just said aloud; then Rouelle believed that the pupil had discovered the arcanum by his own sagacity, and begged him not to divulge what he had himself just told to two hundred persons. One day, when performing an experiment during a lecture, he said to his hearers: "You see, gentlemen, this cauldron over the flame? Well, if I were to leave off stirring it, an explosion would at once occur which would make us all jump." While saying these words, he did not fail to forget to stir, and the prediction was accomplished: the explosion took place with a fearful

1. And make notes so that you can use them. If you will have to include footnotes, be sure to jot down the details you need—at least the author, title, publisher, date, and page numbers. (Each field loves its own footnotes, so you'll have to check books in your specialty to see just how the pros do it.)

noise: the laboratory windows were all smashed, and the audience fled to the garden. [Cesare Lombroso, *The Eccentricities of Famous Men.*]

Cesare Lombroso has found stories that prove some geniuses are sometimes forgetful, but that hardly proves that all are. In addition, he has neglected to spell out why he considers both Rouelle and Newton "geniuses."

Keep asking the question: does this *really* prove my main idea? Or, if not, does it add to that idea so significantly that I ought to rewrite my thesis sentence?

If you mark out a passage, and decide to use it as a quotation, prepare us. Spell out how it applies. Suggest what we are to look for in the passage. Here, for instance, is John Henry Raleigh proving that the life of poor people in nineteenth-century London was rough. He quotes a book from the period, by a man who went out to interview the street people and described their daily lives.

> The life of the London poor in the nineteenth century was, for the most part, miserable, and no one who has read Henry Mayhew, that great sociologist, can ever forget his grim and heartbreaking peoples and scenes. If man had set out consciously to fashion a hell for his fellow men, he could not have done better than nineteenth-century English culture did with the poor who "lived" off the streets of London. Indeed Mayhew's descriptions in *London Labour and the London Poor* sometimes convey a kind of Pandemonium quality and one can almost sniff the sulphur in the air. His description of a crowd entering a "Penny Gaff"—a kind of temporary theater which put on salacious performances—suggests some of the horror.
>
> "Forward they came, bringing an overpowering stench with them, laughing and yelling as they pushed their way through the waiting room. One woman carrying a sickly child with a bulging forehead, was reeling drunk, the saliva running down her mouth as she stared about with a heavy, fixed eye. Two boys were pushing her from side to side, while the poor infant slept, breathing heavily, as if stupefied, through the din. Lads jumping on girls, and girls laughing hysterically from being tickled by the youths behind them, every one shouting and jumping, presented a mad scene of frightful enjoyment." [John Henry Raleigh, *Time, Place, and Idea.*]

By telling us beforehand what we may find in the passage, Raleigh helps us toward what he wants us to find. He also eases us past that white space, and into the quotation. (Many readers jump past all quotations that are set off from the flow of the text. So if you simply string together quotations, without much analysis, readers will decide that you yourself have nothing much to say.)

INTRODUCING

Ponder one of the quotations at the end of this chapter, and write a few sentences stating a main point; then show how certain details in this quotation will support that conclusion. Remember, you are writing an introduction to the passage, not a summary, so suggest why we should read it, rather than giving us a digest.

Your main point: _____

Details: _____

_____

_____

_____

With some subjects, you can actually go out in the streets and talk with people, the way Henry Mayhew did in nineteenth-century London. And when you have interviewed a number of people, you will have a better feel of the topic, and your generalizations about what most people experience will carry weight. Then you can pick a few words from one or two individuals to sum up. Quotations from real people help any argument. Who to talk to differs from one piece of writing to the next, but here are a few of the best targets, and some drawbacks.

- Authorities in the field. (Remember, they disagree, so although your expert says one thing, a reader who knows another authority may cancel yours out.)
- The man in the street. (But then, what does he know?)
- Former employers or users. (What are their biases? Why are they willing to talk?)
- Public relations men. (They are paid to make the boss, and the product, look good.)
- Friends. (Don't they already agree with you? Not too objective.)

Direct testimony and straightforward observations of real actions will make your point better than any book learning. Four Guns, an Oglala Sioux, once had dinner with some white men, including an anthropologist who had been taking notes on the Sioux culture. Four Guns told the white men that their ways were not his. As an example, he stressed the differences he had noticed between the value each culture put on written, as opposed to spoken, knowledge.

> Our host has filled many notebooks with the sayings of our fathers as they came down to us. This is the way of his people; they put great store upon writing; always there is a paper. But we have learned that though there are many papers in Washington upon which are written promises to pay us for our lands, no white man seems to remember them. However, we know our host will not forget what he has written down, and we hope that the white people will read it.
>
> But we are puzzled as to what useful service all this writing serves. Whenever white people come together there is writing. When we go to buy some sugar or tea, we see the white trader busy writing in a book; even the white doctor as he sits beside his patient writes on a piece of paper. The white people must think paper has some mysterious power to help them on in the world. The Indian needs no writings; words that are true sink deep into his heart where they remain; he never forgets them. On the other hand, if the white man loses his papers, he is helpless. I once heard one of their preachers say that no white man was admitted to heaven unless there were writings about him in a great book.

If you want to go beyond texts, step outdoors. Record what you notice there, with all your senses. Again, though, do so with an eye on your larger point. Jane

Jacobs, for instance, draws some general conclusions about what makes a city neighborhood work—then drops down to the street level for a concrete example.

> A good city street neighborhood achieves a marvel of balance between its people's determination to have essential privacy and their simultaneous wishes for differing degrees of contact, enjoyment or help from the people around. This balance is largely made up of small, sensitively managed details, practiced and accepted so casually that they are normally taken for granted.
>
> Perhaps I can best explain this subtle but all-important balance in terms of the stores where people leave keys for their friends, a common custom in New York. [*The Death and Life of Great American Cities.*]

EXERCISE

Thoreau and his brother paddled along the Merrimack River in the early nineteenth century, camping out at night. Even today some of the stretches they covered are wooded and rural. But the split-level ranch houses are moving in, and the drone from highways bounces off the wide river, even at midnight. Read what he wrote (at the end of this chapter) and then think of how you might fit that into some essay of your own—on nature, perhaps, or camping, or human sounds.

What is his main point? (Copy it out here, word for word, if you can find a sentence or phrase that sums it up): ————————————

————————————

————————————

————————————

What is your main point? ————————————

————————————

————————————

In a few sentences, introduce his passage as proof of your main point. Tell us what to look for in Thoreau. You will then have written a paragraph making a point, and setting a context for a quotation that proves your point.

————————————

————————————

————————————

Through numbers and charts, we can sum up hundreds of events and opinions, but most of us distrust statistics. We ask: who says? What are these numbers based on? (In sum, what's the hidden bias?) How many people were sampled? What mathematical hocus-pocus has been done to the raw data, to come out with those percentages?

Cast doubt on your opponent's figures by suggesting their motives for under-

or overestimating. Henry Mayhew thought prostitution much more widespread than the police would admit; for evidence, he turned to numbers:

> To show how difficult it is to give from any data at present before the public anything like a correct estimate of the number of prostitutes in London, we may mention (extracting from the work of Dr. Ryan) that while the Bishop of Exeter asserted the number of prostitutes in London to be 80,000, the City Police stated to Dr. Ryan that it did not exceed 7,000 to 8,000. About the year 1793 Mr. Colquhon, a police magistrate, concluded, after tedious investigations, that there were 50,000 prostitutes in this metropolis. At that period, the population was one million, and as it is now more than double we may form some idea of the extensive ramifications of this insidious vice. . . .
> We have before stated the assumed number of prostitutes in London to be about 80,000 and large as this total may appear, it is not improbable that it is below the reality rather than above it. [*Those that Will not Work,* Vol. IV of *London Labour and the London Poor.*]

Mayhew adds, subtracts, and works out his own equation. But if you do not find any single statistic that makes your point that clearly, you may want to mention a whole passel of them. This tends to overawe—as in this passage by Steve Gaines.

> Inside the disc jockey's booth the sight of the main control board pleased him. It was like the control panel of a spaceship: knobs, keys, buttons, levers, an elaborate mixing board, with 16 pots, 15,000 watts of Teac amplifiers, a keyboard for playing the lights manually and a computer synthesizer to play them automatically.
> Three turntables, imbedded in lucite stands, hung from thick rubber strips which absorbed vibrations. The playing arms lay delicately at rest, a battery-powered spotlight cutting across the surface of each turntable for easy cue lighting. Cameron touched a tiny metal switch on the front of the panel and the board lighted up, twinkling below him like an electronic Christmas tree. He ran his hands lovingly over the board, the knobs and switches tickling his palms. The best set of electric trains ever. [*Discotheque.*]

The numbers blitz us like strobe lights—flashy, but not too informative, this "evidence" helps build a mood, but not a thought. So either boil the numbers down to a few bold totals, or organize them around some idea that carries an emotional charge. Otherwise, you make the reader's eyes glaze over.

Proverbs, too, are tempting as evidence. They represent years of peasant wisdom, right? Yes, but . . . they are cliches; they make you sound like a finger-pointing nanny. Nothing in excess.

Rules and laws also carry the force of popular opinion—and social pressure. If you can quote any regulation that applies, your reader must buck Authority before he can disagree with you. But then, that is why we hire lawyers. To an innocent, the United States Constitution sounds clear, but the Supreme Court guarantees that even this law behind the laws lies open to new interpretation.

A blend of evidence works best, implying that authority, and numbers, and folk wisdom back up what your interviews, your books, and your direct observations show. The more evidence—to a point—the better. That point, of course, wavers.

It depends on who you are writing for, how important facts are to them, how much you need to persuade them—a whole range of considerations that we will look at in the chapter on "Who Are You Writing For." But for the moment, assume you have an intuitive sense of that.

I suggest you write at length the first time through, then sit back and weigh the evidence. Then cut out the weakest examples by applying these guidelines:

- Is this evidence clearly related to the point?
- Does it, in fact, prove my point?
- If so, does it provide evidence that I have not already given? (Is this new evidence? Is it a new *type* of evidence?)
- If not new, does it deepen the emotional force of what I say?
- If not new, and not somehow significant, is there any reason at all for including it?

Evidence expands and contracts, depending on the impression you want to make. The more you want to overwhelm, the more evidence you will quote; the more you want to be clear, the more you will restrain yourself, limiting yourself to what you have heard and seen directly, short passages from your reading, simple statistics, and, of course, afterthoughts.

In *Roughing It,* in order to prove that the waters of Lake Tahoe were so clear the boat seemed to be floating on air, Mark Twain mentioned particular physical details he could see, not just from twenty, but from eighty feet. (Statistics!) He told a story about riding over a boulder, only to find it was much deeper than they thought. But then he added another claim: that the water was not just transparent, but brilliant; that objects could be seen not just as clearly as through air, but better. Here is something new. Then he rounded out his argument by calling these boat excursions "balloon voyages," a reminder of the original claim that they seemed to be floating in air—but now that air is much brighter.

So when you feel the need for more material, remember that there are three kinds available: live, frozen, and dead. When you talk to someone, or go yourself to describe an event, your evidence brings with it the fresh air of your own existence. When you go through old books, statistical charts, law codes, you find life caught in midstep: convincing, but often chilly, and much less warm than your own observations. And when you force yourself to put down every possible fact and example and number that could prove your case, you risk killing off the whole point. Pedantry kills by boring from within.

To fend off that disease, ponder these questions as you look for more evidence:

What is my own main point?

Do I really need to say anything more?

MORE EVIDENCE

SO singularly clear was the water, that where it was only twenty or thirty feet deep the bottom was so perfectly distinct that the boat seemed floating in the air! Yes, where it was even *eighty* feet deep. Every little pebble was distinct, every speckled trout, every hand's breadth of sand. Often, as we lay on our faces, a granite boulder, as large as a village church, would start out of the bottom apparently, and seem climbing up rapidly to the surface, till presently it threatened to touch our faces, and we could not resist the impulse to seize an oar and avert the danger. But the boat would float on, and the boulder descend again, and then we could see that when we had been exactly above it, it must still have been twenty or thirty feet below the surface. Down through the transparency of these great depths, the water was not *merely* transparent, but dazzlingly, brilliantly so. All objects seen through it had a bright, strong vividness, not only of outline, but of every minute detail, which they would not have had when seen simply through the same depth of atmosphere. So empty and airy did all spaces seem below us, and so strong was the sense of floating high aloft in mid-nothingness, that we called these boat excursions "balloon voyages." [Mark Twain, *Roughing It.*]

FOR the most part there was no recognition of human life in the night, no human breathing was heard, only the breathing of the wind. As we sat up, kept awake by the novelty of our situation, we heard at intervals foxes stepping about over the dead leaves and brushing the dewy grass close to our tent, and once a muskrat fumbling among the potatoes and melons in our boat, which when we hastened to the shore we could detect only a ripple in the water ruffling the disk of a star. At intervals we were serenaded by the song of a dreaming sparrow or the throttled cry of an owl, but after each sound which near at hand broke the stillness of the night, each crackling of the twigs, or rustling among the leaves, there was a sudden pause, and deeper and more conscious silence, as if the intruder were aware that no life was rightfully abroad at that hour. There was a fire in Lowell, as we judged, this night, and we saw the horizon blazing, and heard the distant alarm bells, as it were a faint tinkling music borne to these woods. But the most constant and memorable sound of a summer's night, which we did not fail to hear every night afterward, though at no time so incessantly and so favorably as now, was the barking of the house dogs, from the loudest and hoarsest bark to the faintest aerial palpitation under the eaves of heaven, from the patient but anxious mastiff to the timid and wakeful terrier, at first loud and rapid, then faint and slow, to be imitated only in a whisper: wowo-wow-wow-wow-wo-wo-w-w. [Henry Thoreau, *A Week on the Concord and Merrimack Rivers.*]

INSURANCE companies have statistical data which state that men whose only goal is to retire will die within eighteen months after achieving that goal.

In talking with retired men, a common problem is that suddenly they feel they have nothing to look forward to, or as one man put it: "When I was working, I always looked forward to my weekends and summer vacations, and I don't have that to look forward to anymore." A friend mentioned to a recently retired man that now he could do all the things he'd always wanted to do, to which the newly retired man replied, "All I ever wanted to do was work." [Ken Olson, *Hey Man, Open Up and Live!*]

9th DAY:

Distinguishing Parts

You begin writing, and you find that nothing follows. You have this to say, and that, and the other thing, and you can hardly write one sentence before some completely different idea pops up.

Or your subject seems like a big lump, and whenever you chop off one hunk to write about, other sections ooze out.

What to do?

Spring cleaning.

Distinguish the elements you are dealing with. Sort them out in order of time, or space, or logic. And if you try all those organizing principles, and none work, simply classify the parts of your subject in separate sections.

Doing this helps the reader several ways:

    1. You do not ask him to understand everything at once.

    2. You give him a way to organize many different facts.

    3. You let him feel forward movement.

For example, when the composer Aaron Copland began to talk about the way we listen to music, he realized that many people experience confusion when they try to analyze or understand the process. So Copland divided listening into three levels—three ways in which we listen. One is just sensuous—what our ear likes. Another is expressive: what the music means to us, what it reminds us of. And the third is more technical: we analyze the music as music, the way a professional might.

> We all listen to music according to our separate capacities. But for the sake of analysis, the whole listening process may become clearer if we break it up into its component parts, so to speak. In a certain sense we all listen to music on three separate planes. For lack of a better terminology, we might name these: (1) the sensuous plane, (2) the expressive plane, (3) the sheerly musical plane. The only advantage to be gained from mechanically splitting up the listening process into these hypothetical planes is the clear view to be had of the way in which we listen. [*What to Listen for in Music.*]

And when Thomas Hobbes tried to analyze what makes us go to war, he turned to our human character:

So that in the nature of man we find three principal causes of quarrel. First, competition; secondly, difference; thirdly, glory.

The first makes men invade for gain; the second for safety; and the third for reputation. The first use violence to make themselves masters of other men's persons, wives, children, and cattle; the second, to defend them; the third, for trifles, as a word, a smile, a different opinion, and any other sign of undervalue, either direct in their persons, or by reflection in their kindred, their friends, their nation, their profession or their name. [*Leviathan.*]

Numbering, then, does help separate ideas that tend to blur together. But is there any logic to the numbering? Sometimes not. And when there is not, we come away feeling somehow cheated.

For numbers imply a hierarchy. When we see them, we imagine they are going to lead us through stages, from first to last. Or from lowest to highest. Or from prime ideas to the more numerous but less important ones. In fact, we long for some such progression.

Below, for instance, is a bad way of classifying. The writers have been so browbeaten by their subject that they have simply numbered a bunch of ideas, without indicating why one should naturally come before the next. Result: a bland motionlessness.

Cooking involves 1) taste factors 2) menu planning 3) cutting and slicing 4) preparation 5) place settings 6) application of heat 7) mixing ingredients and 8) sensible shopping.

If the authors had made these numbered phrases into sentences, we might have been able to spot the reasoning behind this order. How does one lead to the next? As is, the list just gives us ideas, in no obvious progression. Result: we can hardly feel we are moving forward, as our eyes drop down the page.

So when you start jotting down lists, consider what really should go first. See if your ideas can fit into any of these patterns suggested by time, space, logic, or value:

1. What comes first, then what, and then what . . .
2. What place do you go to first, and then where . . .
3. What fact do you have to establish first, in order to prove what, which in turn proves . . .
4. What is the most valuable, next most valuable . . .

TEN FINGER EXERCISES

Fill in the blanks with ten things you do with your hands. Then put numbers in the two columns. Under *Time,* write a one (1) next to the first thing you do in the day, two (2) next to the next, and so on. Under *Value,* write down a one (1) next to the activity you value most, down to ten (10), the one you value least.

Things Done	Time	Value
_____		
_____		
_____		
_____		

_____

_____

_____

_____

_____

_____

When we move forward in time, setting out an event in stages, a reader gets an accelerated sense of growth. We can watch the sun come up and set in a sentence, or the world take form in a paragraph. If the phases are clearly distinguished, our pleasure in this development increases. Phrases like *at the beginning,* and *then,* and *now* mark out such stages almost as clearly as numbers could—and with less interruption. Here, for instance, T.H. Everett, of the New York Botanical Gardens, describes how to divide up a fern, to start new plants:

> The best time to divide is just as new growth begins; when, after a period of comparative rest, roots are becoming busy and new shoots are about to pop. Don't wait until these latter are half-grown or even well advanced. Act as soon as you see them *beginning* to grow. Most plants start their new growth cycles in late winter or spring.
>
> A few hours prior to dividing, soak the plant in water. At operating time, spread the fingers of one hand over the top of its pot and between or around the shoots; turn it upside down; take hold of the bottom of the pot with the other hand, and tap the pot's rim sharply on the edge of a bench or table. This will remove the plant from its container.
>
> Now decide upon the most effective means of separating the clump before you into pieces. [*How to Grow Beautiful House Plants.*]

Elisabeth Kübler-Ross wants to prove that in earlier generations people did not flinch from death, did not hide it from their children, and did not force the dying person out of the home during the last moments.

> I remember as a child the death of a farmer. He fell from a tree and was not expected to live. He asked simply to die at home, a wish that was granted without questioning. He called his daughters into the bedroom and spoke with each one of them alone for a few minutes. He arranged his affairs quietly, though he was in great pain, and distributed his belongings and his land, none of which was to be split until his wife should follow him in death. He also asked each of his children to share in the work, duties, and tasks that he had carried on until the time of the accident. He asked his friends to visit him once more, to bid goodbye to them. Although I was a small child at the time, he did not exclude me or my siblings. We were allowed to share in the preparations of the family just as we were permitted to grieve with them until he died. When he did die, he was left at home, in his own beloved home which he had built, and among his friends and neighbors who went to take a last look at him where he lay in the midst of flowers in the place he had lived in and loved so much. [*On Death and Dying.*]

We can follow that man, moment to moment, to death. And that way we feel nothing has been hidden from us: her point.

Our common sense sorts things out spatially, too. Here is how a lone rider discovers a western valley:

> Riding on, he studied the valley. To right and left lay towering ridges that walled the valley in and to the east other peaks lifted, and west the valley swung hard around and at one corner the wall was broken sharply off to fall sheer away for more than six hundred feet. Kilkenny paused long upon the lip, looking out over that immeasurable distance toward the faraway line of the purple hills. It was then that he first became conscious of the sound, a faint scarcely discernible whispering. Holding himself erect, he listened intently. It was the wind! The whispering wind!
>
> Wind among the tall pines, among the torcs and the erosion-gnawed holes, a sound such as he had never heard, a sound like far-off music in which no notes could be detected, a sound so strange that he could not stop listening. He turned then in his saddle and looked back over the valley he had found. At least two thousand acres! [Louis L'Amour, *Kilkenny*.]

L'Amour has taken us on a tour of the valley, directing our attention north, south, east, and west, forward and back, surveying the whole. In effect, he has set up signposts, telling us when to look down and up, left and right, out and back.

Those signposts—we use them when organizing any such material—can help distinguish the sections of our discussion making it easier to plow through. Here, for instance, is Mark Twain describing the Washoe Zephyr, a dust storm that blew down on Carson City, Nevada. Twain starts in the upper air, proceeds a shade lower; lower still; drops by levels down to a grade only thirty or forty feet above the ground. Perhaps he exaggerates, but his observations seem so clear we can agree with his argument that the Washoe wind is "no trifling matter."

> That was all we saw that day, for it was two o'clock, now, and according to custom the daily "Washoe Zephyr" set in: a soaring dust-drift about the size of the United States set up edgewise came with it, and the capital of Nevada Territory disappeared from view. Still, there were sights to be seen which were not wholly uninteresting to newcomers; for the vast dust cloud was thickly freckled with things strange to the upper air—things living and dead, that flitted hither and thither, going and coming, appearing and disappearing among the rolling billows of dust—hats, chickens and parasols sailing in the remote heavens; blankets, tin signs, sage brush and shingles a shade lower; door mats and buffalo robes lower still; shovels and coal scuttles on the next grade; glass doors, cats and little children on the next; disrupted lumber yards, light buggies and wheel barrows on the next; and down only thirty or forty feet above ground was a scurrying storm of emigrating rooves and vacant lots.
>
> It was something to see that much. I could have seen more, if I could have kept the dust out of my eyes. [*Roughing It.*]

Twain sets up signposts to get us from level to level. He also moves from the possible to the absurd in his levels. However if you organize your material around fairly logical claims, then you may want to move from the trivial to the important. Abe Lincoln had listened to a lot of arguments in favor of slavery, and he wrote notes to himself, trying to puzzle out why each one was wrong. He started with the silliest, and ended with the most revealing:

If A can prove, however conclusively, that he may, of right, enslave B, why may not B snatch the same argument, and prove equally, that he may enslave A?—You say A is white and B is black. It is *color,* then; the lighter, having the right to enslave the darker? Take care. By this rule, you are to be slave to the first man you meet, with a fairer skin than your own. You do not mean *color* exactly?—You mean the whites are *intellectually* the superiors of the blacks, and, therefore, have the right to enslave them? Take care again. By this rule, you are to be slave to the first man you meet, with an intellect superior to your own. But, say you, it is a question of *interest;* and, if you can make it your *interest,* you have the right to enslave another. Very well. And if he can make it his interest, he has the right to enslave you.

The signposts of logic are there: if . . . then . . . why . . . however. Lincoln thus dismisses his opponents' poor logic while moving toward a real explanation of the reason they talk that way: it is in their economic interest to keep slaves. He has arranged his own thoughts on a ladder of value.

That puts me in mind of his letter to General McClellan, who had come up with a lousy plan for attacking Richmond during the Civil War. Notice the way Lincoln's arguments follow an ascending scale of values.

If you will give me satisfactory answers to the following questions, I shall gladly yield my plan to yours. Does not your plan involve a greatly larger expenditure of *time,* and *money* than mine? Wherein is a victory *more certain* by your plan than mine? Wherein is a victory *more valuable* by your plan than mine? In fact, would it not be *less* valuable, in this, that it would break no great line of the enemy's communications, while mine would? In case of disaster, would not a retreat be more difficult by your plan than mine?

A SIGNIFICANT EXERCISE

Think of someone whose political ideas you despise. State his position in a sentence, then refute it just as quickly. Do this on three or four issues. Just write them down as they occur to you. Only then consider order. In the right-hand corner of each, put one (1) for least significant, and move up to the most significant.

_____

_____

_____

_____

Once you know your method of organization, you can recall the typical signposts. Here are some examples, to start you off.

TIME:	SPACE:	LOGIC:	VALUE:
before	nearby	therefore	more
after	farther off	however	less
then	above	hence	significantly
slowly	beyond	furthermore	most important

To sum up:
1. Use a pattern that develops in time, space, logic, or value.
2. Distinguish the parts.
3. Use signposts.
4. Emphasize movement.

You need not go too far in distinguishing parts. Link what ought to be linked within each paragraph, as suggested in the chapter "Unifying." And condense the key points, as in "Summing Up." Look past the signposts to the goal, and we will go faster.

If you have figured out a reasonable progression, a real movement through the material, then the signposts will simply emphasize our speed. Once you have used common sense to order the facts, you can accelerate our understanding.

Open up your subject. Count its parts, time its stages, map out its subdivisions, argue through its logic to some inescapable point.

NEAT DISTINCTIONS

WOOD burns in three distinct phases. Even in well-seasoned wood that has been dried over twelve months, some water remains. Some of the water is chemically combined with the wood, but most is free water. When the wood burns, this free water is driven off as steam, which is generally speaking, the white smoke. The second phase of burning is the breakdown of the wood into charcoal and the release of the volatile gases and liquids that are in the wood. Finally, the charcoal itself burns—this produces most of the heat. This is the natural three-stage process of burning a fire outdoors and in fireplaces. In wood stoves, these three phases occur simultaneously. [Allen A. Swenson, *Wood Heat.*]

A WORKMAN not educated to this business, nor acquainted with the use of the machinery employed in it, could scarce, perhaps, with his utmost industry, make one pin in a day, and certainly could not make twenty. But in the way in which this business is now carried on, not only the whole work is a peculiar trade, but it is divided into a number of branches, of which the greater part are likewise peculiar trades. One man draws out the wire, another straights it, a third cuts it, a fourth points it, a fifth grinds it at the top for receiving the head; to make the head requires three distinct operations; to put it on is a peculiar business, to whiten the pins is another; it is even a trade by itself to put them into the paper; and the important business of making a pin is, in this manner, divided into about eighteen distinct operations, which in some manufactories, are all performed by distinct hands, though in others the same man will sometimes perform two or three of them. [Adam Smith, *The Wealth of Nations.*]

CRAFTY men condemn studies; simple men admire them; and wise men use them. . . . Read not to contradict and confute; nor to believe and take for granted; nor to find talk and discourse; but to weigh and consider. Some books are to be tasted, others to be swallowed, and some few to be chewed and digested; that is, some books are to be read only in parts; others to be read, but not curiously; and some few to be read wholly, and with diligence and attention. [Francis Bacon, "Of Studies."]

10th DAY

Who Is Your Audience?

When you do not think about the person you are writing for, you tend to write for an ideal teacher from the past, or some composite of authorities. You may secretly resent all their criticism, and gradually anger may creep into your writing—a bitterness that the reader may feel is directed at him. Such anger shows up when you insult the reader, or tell jokes he thinks are in bad taste, or refer to events he has never heard of, or oversimplify subjects he already has an expert knowledge of.

But when you know who you are writing for—in detail, and with sympathy—you can shape your writing so that the reader can understand it, without struggling. You can move him by paying attention to your own emotions. You can provide him with the ideas he wants, and the evidence to back them up.

As you read this, for instance, you can sense my attitude toward you. As my mood changes, you pick that up. If I get mad at you, you may back off. If I coddle you, you may throw the book down. But, intuitively, you get a feeling for how I feel about you. Somehow, my attitude toward you affects my writing, shows up in it, stains the communication.

But how can I have an opinion of you, when I've never met you?

Well, I've tried to imagine you. I've thought about your age, occupation, motives, tastes, values. And once I got an impression of you (putting together a number of people I know, stressing some traits), I wondered about my own character. What exactly do I want to do to—or for—you? Do I want to help you or beat you? Do I want you to love me? Respect me? Obey me? Or am I more interested in hearing that you've grown by grappling with this book?

My ideas of you—and my attitudes toward you—have a stronger impact on my way of talking than any technique could. In fact, a writer's emotional stance toward the reader often leads to a style that makes understanding difficult—or easy.

For instance, if I am angry at you, even subconsciously, I may beat you with statistics, talk in terms that make you feel dumb, strut around as an authority. I might get incoherent, and slam you with half-thought-out images and slogans. Or I might use frosty horrible politeness, to show you I'm better than you, as in this Dear John letter typical of nineteenth-century propriety:

My dear friend,

It is with the greatest reluctance that I feel I must terminate our relationship. Recent events, of which we both are painfully aware, have indicated to me in clear and compelling terms that our natures are essentially incompatible and our viewpoints on many crucial issues too completely dissimilar. While your companionship in the past has brought me moments of joy, which I shall treasure eternally, I feel it would be injudicious on both our parts to prolong a relationship which, it has become increasingly clear, is not based on mutual trust and respect. Please extend to your dear mother my best wishes for a speedy and quick recovery from her untimely accident.

Sincerely, Alberta

If I am afraid of you, I clam up. Each sentence stiffens. My vocabulary chokes in my throat. If I'm really scared, my fingers may tremble so much I don't write anything.

If I want you to love me, I may fall down pleading, get up boasting, spout violent cliches, cringe, pose, or write beautiful, poetic lyrics.

But if I think of writing for you as just a day's work, my tone may fade to neutral; I may be clear, but a bit bland. Try to take an emotional stance in the following exercise:

TABLE TALK

Write "Pass the cream" . . .

Angrily: ————————————————————————————

————————————————————————————

Fearfully: ————————————————————————————

————————————————————————————

With excessive politeness: ————————————————————————

————————————————————————————

Why analyze the reader, then? To help the mind focus on your audience, so that when you begin to write, your words will home in on their interests, tastes, and values. So that you can write at their intellectual level, without sneering or trying to impress and at the emotional level they expect, without forcing yourself to feel what you don't. Also, to keep negative feelings from getting in the way.

Here are some questions you could ask yourself about your reader. Sometimes you know the exact person who will read what you write; if so, then use these questions to isolate what the "reader" in him or her expects from your writing. Sometimes you have only a vague notion of your audience; in that case, explore your own half-formed ideas of these people, groping for friends who are like that, noting what you like and dislike about them, figuring out how they think—in effect, construct a picture of them.

What is your image of your reader?

- What do you think he wants, from what you write?
- What does he want, in general, out of life?
- What is his taste in furniture? Food? Fun?

- In reading material?
- How does he talk?
- What ideas does he want to find in your writing?
- What conclusions?
- What evidence?
- What level of intellectual effort will he put into reading?
- Does he expect his emotions to be stirred?
- Which ones?
- How smart is he?
- How big a vocabulary does he have?
- How many ideas can he grasp at one sitting?
- Does he pick up new ideas quickly?

SKETCHING YOUR READER

Using these questions, and following up any other thoughts that occur to you, describe one person (not several) who will read your next piece of writing. If you do not know this person, make up a character and invent a name.

    As you might imagine, each trait you discover in your reader raises some answering emotion in you. You are like him in this, you disapprove of that, you envy another characteristic. In some ways, you are—even though it takes place in your own mind—developing a relationship with the reader. You are gradually working out a stance toward him—and a tone you want to take toward him. This may be intuitive, but intuitive understanding can be talked about: more dangerous are purely unconscious attitudes, for these rise up without your recognizing them, and make your voice shake when you mean it to sound strong, or make you seem to snarl when you think you are just being polite. So, still thinking of the reader you've sketched above, ponder these questions.

- Do you really want to give the reader what he wants?
- In what areas do you want to go beyond that?
- Are you tempted to shock the reader with truth?
- Do you see yourself sweet-talking the reader?
- Do you think you know more than the reader?
- Do you think you're basically smarter?
- If so, do you think in terms of pulling him "up to" your level?
- Or are you going to write down to him?
- Are you going to appeal to his emotions?
- If so, which ones?
- Are these feelings you also have?
- Or are you trying to arouse emotions in him, without having them yourself?
- Do you think your reader is better than you?

- In what way? Smarter, richer, etc.?
- How will you handle his being better?
- Will you pretend to be well-informed when you are not?
- Will you pretend to care more than you do?
- Will you bull, to cover up your ignorance?

THE WRITER'S SECRETS

In order to find an image that sums up what writing for your particular reader means to you, first, envision a simple action that parallels what you feel about talking to him (sharpening a pencil, drinking coffee).

_____

Now think of your relationship with your reader; how do you sum it up? ____

_____

What parts of your life do you think you would not mention, as not interesting to, or expected by that reader? _____

_____

In omitting these experiences, would you then be playing a part, or posing? If so, what role would you play? _____

_____

 Confusion arises when we claim to be one thing, but feel we are another: often, both messages come through and cause static. The reader, for instance, may hear you saying you care about his problems, but he may get a strange feeling that you want to add to his troubles. Or you may feel so intimidated by the reader's power and wisdom that you write as if he could see connections between different events without your making them. By pretending to be an expert writing for an expert, you may have lost him. Or if you just hate to do the report, you may load it with jargon, to punish the person who assigned it, knowing they cannot follow this insider's talk.

 In reaction to such mixed signals, readers often cry out that they are "confused" or "bored." Actually they are not so confused. They often see pretty clearly what you are up to (even if they can't follow the details of your argument). They just don't like it. Or you. (Beware of the reader who tells you how impressed he was with your report, and how complicated it seemed. He probably stopped reading it in the middle. Perhaps he felt put off by the way you wrote it. But maybe you meant him to be.)

 How can you avoid causing the reader such confusion and resentment?

 First of all, show that you really do understand his questions, his problems. For example, you might be able to sum up his attitudes in a few paragraphs, to give him credit, even if you then go on to disagree. If you can state his position without sarcasm, he will feel you understand what he wants said—and then he will feel much kindlier toward what you have to say.

 Showing the reader you share his doubts can help, too. Or his worries. Or his own mixed feelings about some current controversy.

SIMPATICO

Write down two of your ideas that you feel sure your reader strongly agrees with. Then put down one you are certain he would find offensive.

1. _____

2. _____

3. _____

Question: would you mention the offensive idea to your reader? _____

Another way to avoid giving a reader a bellyache is to understand your own real feelings about the subject, and about your reader—and let them show. That approach is not always appropriate: you could get fired for being honest. But if you feel it is appropriate, let your emotions hang out, even if you suspect they may upset the reader for a moment. For instance, Mao Tse-tung knew that some of his readers did not want a violent revolution in China, but he disagreed—and he let them know it.

> A revolution is not a dinner party, or writing an essay, or painting a picture, or doing embroidery; it cannot be so refined, so leisurely and gentle, so temperate, kind, courteous, restrained and magnanimous. A revolution is an insurrection, an act of violence by which one class overthrows another. A rural revolution is a revolution by which the peasantry overthrows the power of the feudal landlord class. Without using the greatest force, the peasants cannot possibly overthrow the deep-rooted authority of the landlords which has lasted for thousands of years. [*Investigation of Peasant Movement in Hunan.*]

If you do not dare to come right out with what you think, you'll have to work twice as hard to keep it from showing through in spite of yourself. And all that sweat may make your work stink of effort and mendacity.

Once you have understood who your reader is, and how you feel about him, the real question is: can you be friendly? If not, you may be writing for the wrong person.

To sum up, there are a thousand questions you could ask about yourself and about your potential reader, all designed to make sure that what you write is really aimed at that reader's interests, tastes, values, mind, and emotions. And if that upsets you too much, why write for someone like that?

So before you write—and whenever you find yourself bogging down, postponing, or woolgathering—ponder all the issues behind these simple questions:

1. *Who is my reader?*
2. *What are my real feelings toward that reader?*
3. *Do I intend to let my opinions show?*

ABOUT READERS

SUPPOSE you are the perfect reader of this book. You have read carefully every word I wrote up to this point, you have studied all the examples, you have worked all the exercises. You are thoroughly conscious by now of what makes for simplicity. You measure your sentences, count your affixes, and bring in people wherever you can. You know how to use the yardstick formula and are master of the little tricks of using verbs or avoiding commenting adjectives and empty words. You have learned how to be neither rhetorical nor pedantic. In short, you got the theory of plain talk cold. Now you want to practice.

To do that, you want to know where to find *very easy* English, *easy* English, *fairly easy* English, and so on up the scale, and what kind of language to use for what kind of people. [Rudolf Flesch, "Talking Down and Reading Up," *The Art of Plain Talk.*]

IT is the spectator, not life, that art really mirrors. [Oscar Wilde.]

THE only thing I owe the public is a good performance. [Humphrey Bogart.]

IF the reader will excuse me, I will say nothing of my antecedents, nor of the circumstances which led me to leave my native country; the narrative would be tedious to him and painful to myself. Suffice it, that when I left home it was with the intention of going to some new colony, and either finding, or even perhaps purchasing, waste crown land suitable for cattle or sheep farming, by which means I thought that I could better my fortunes more rapidly than in England.

It will be seen that I did not succeed in my design, and that however much I may have met with what was new and strange, I have been unable to reap any pecuniary advantage.

It is true, I imagine myself to have made a discovery which, if I can be the first to profit by it, will bring me a recompense beyond all money computation, and secure me a position such as has not been attained by more than some fifteen or sixteen persons since the creation of the universe. But to this end I must possess myself of a considerable sum of money; neither do I know how to get it, except by interesting the public in my story, and inducing the charitable to come forward and assist me. With this hope I now publish my adventures; but I do so with great reluctance, for I fear that my story will be doubted unless I tell the whole of it; and yet I dare not do so, lest others with more means than mine should get the start of me. I prefer the risk of being doubted to that of being anticipated, and have therefore concealed my destination on leaving England, as also the point from which I began my more serious and difficult journey.

My chief consolation lies in the fact that truth bears its own impress, and that my story will carry conviction by reason of the internal evidence for its accuracy. No one who is himself honest will doubt my being so. [Samuel Butler, *Erewhon.*]

11th DAY

Being More Human

In schools and businesses, we are often taught—by implication and by direct command—not to use the word *I*, not to mention particular people by name, in fact, to edit out what makes life intriguing.

But that rule makes writing no better than an impersonal bulletin sent by one machine to another machine, without a mind between. And such reports create an eerie world, in which . . .

- No one does anything: things occur, and no one is to blame—or *one* is, that nameless creature of anonymity.
- Events make themselves happen.
- Reports appear without anyone creating them.
- Conclusions get reached by unknown agents.
- Classes of living organisms parade in patterns, but not one person with a name or a point of view.

A metal world.

To be more human:

- Take a clear, personal stand.
- Say *I*—and *you*.
- Let your own feelings show.
- Use *he, she, him, her,* and *who*.
- Avoid *one*.
- Put down names.
- Mention family and social relationships.
- Go beyond categories: show what specific people in that category really do, and say.

If you follow these suggestions when you write, I will be able to tell what you think, how you disagree with someone else (and I'll know who); I'll sense your feelings; I'll know where I stand with you.

Of course you have to make generalizations. But you can quickly flesh those out with details (who said what, and why, and what that person did, and what someone else did). For instance, when Mao Tse-tung was young, he went into the Chinese province of Hunan to report on the peasant uprisings there. He heard some cautious peasants claim that the poorer ones were going too far, but he disagreed. He raised the question, said what the peasants actually did, then argued that the peasants had suffered so much, and watched the landlords so long, that the punishments fit the crimes. Read this paragraph, and see if you can "see" what went on—and what Mao thinks.

> Then there is another section of people who say, "Yes, peasant associations are necessary, but they are going rather too far." This is the opinion of the middle-of-the-roaders. But what is the actual situation? True, the peasants are in a sense "unruly" in the countryside. Supreme in authority, the peasant association allows the landlord no say and sweeps away his prestige. This amounts to striking the landlord down to the dust and keeping him there. The peasants threaten, "We will put you in the other register!" They fine the local tyrants and evil gentry, they demand contributions from them, and they smash their sedan-chairs. People swarm into the houses of local tyrants and evil gentry who are against the peasant association, slaughter their pigs and consume their grain. They even loll for a minute or two on the ivory-inlaid beds belonging to the young ladies in the households of the local tyrants and evil gentry. At the slightest provocation they make arrests, crown the arrested with tall paper hats, and parade them through the villages, saying, "You dirty landlords, now you know who we are!" Doing whatever they like and turning everything upside down, they have created a kind of terror in the countryside. This is what some people call "going too far," or "exceeding the proper limits in righting a wrong," or "really too much." Such talk may seem plausible, but in fact it is wrong. First, the local tyrants, evil gentry and lawless landlords have themselves driven the peasants to this. For ages they have used their power to tyrannize over the peasants and trample them underfoot; that is why the peasants have reacted so strongly. The most violent revolts and the most serious disorders have invariably occurred in places where the local tyrants, evil gentry and lawless landlords perpetrated the worst outrages. The peasants are clear-sighted. Who is bad and who is not, who is the worst and who is not quite so vicious, who deserves severe punishment and who deserves to be let off lightly—the peasants keep clear accounts, and very seldom has the punishment exceeded the crime. [*Investigation of Peasant Movement in Hunan.*]

Mao could have left us with his generalizations about class war, evil gentry, and so on, but he has given us pictures of what actually went on, facts he knows some people find embarrassing. By letting his own class hatred show, without disguise, he adds energy to his evidence.

Again, a so-called "objective" writer might have reported "Disk jockey James Runyon died yesterday of cancer, aged 43." But columnist Bob Greene felt more grief than that, and let us see what came to his mind, as the news sank in:

> Someone called the other day to say that Jim Runyon had died. The news was about three weeks old, but I had not heard; no one writes obituaries about a disk jockey. Jim died in Cleveland, I heard, and as soon as I learned about it, I found it hard to think about anything else for the next few hours. I never knew Runyon, at least in the sense that I never met him or shook his hand, but I thought that I should say something about his life, anyway.
>
> I heard that he was 43 years old, and that cancer had done it to him. His name probably means something to some people in Chicago, because he played rock-and-roll records on WCFL here for a couple of years. But when I thought of Runyon, my mind went back to the summer of 1964, and I started hearing his voice again. . . .

This may not be the way things should be, but when I think back to that part of my life, I do not think about a schoolteacher I had, or a book I read, or a movie I saw. Instead, I think about cruising around the lakes in a steamy blue Ford with my friends, turning KYW up all the way and listening to the music and the jocks. We did not think in terms of anyone dying, not then; the idea of Jim Runyon, who called his show "The Runyon Room" and told us that he was "a Runyon named Jim," being dead was too distant to even cross our minds. [Bob Greene, *Johnny Deadline, Reporter.*]

A FACTUAL REPORT

As an exercise, write a one-paragraph obituary for someone you knew as a kid. Include only public information, leave out any personal memories. Then, in a few paragraphs, write down what that person did with you, to you, for you, near you.

_____

_____

_____

_____

If I write about an action as if it is just "done"—with no one doing it—a reader may feel confused and excluded. So whenever you describe an activity, ask yourself: who, really, is doing this? Isn't it a human being? And who am I talking to?

A typical book on business writing, for instance, talks as if no one knows what *classifying* means. And indeed, in their prose, no human does it.

> *Classification of data:* Classification is the sorting of data into homogenous groups. The aim, in essence, is to keep like data together so that they may be more easily dealt with and their relationship established. The alternative is an undigested and disorganized mass of material that represents the writer's confusion and eventually leads to the reader's. [J. Harold Janis, Howard R. Dressner, *Business Writing.*]

GOING PERSONAL

Rewrite the passage freely, inserting as many personal words as you can (*I, me, you, he, she*). Break the clotted ideas down into individual sentences, if you need to. I'll start you off: When I classify, I sort . . . _____

_____

_____

_____

_____

An energetic engineer might be able to describe panning gold in a way that left out the real miner on his knees in the stream: "Gold particles wash down from the original rock in a fan shape; by careful sifting, one can locate the source by defining the fan, and noting the narrow neck." One can. But I miss any feeling for what actually goes on when a prospector pans for gold, and I feel the author is not talking to me, but to himself, or heaven. Here, by contrast, is Mark Twain. He goes from the general to the personal in his second sentence:

> Pocket hunting is an ingenious process. You take a spadeful of earth from the hillside and put it in a large tin pan and dissolve and wash it gradually away till nothing is left but a teaspoon of fine sediment. Whatever gold was in that earth has remained, because, being the heaviest, it has sought the bottom. Among the sediment you will find half a dozen yellow particles no larger than pin-heads. You are delighted. You move off to one side and wash another pan. If you find gold again, you move to one side further, and wash a third pan. If you find *no* gold this time, you are delighted again, because you know you are on the right scent. You lay an imaginary plan, shaped like a fan, with its handle up the hill—for just where the end of the handle is, you argue that the rich deposit lies hidden, whose vagrant grains of gold have escaped and been washed down the hill, spreading farther and farther apart as they wandered. And so you proceed up the hill, washing the earth and narrowing your lines every time the absence of gold in the pan shows that you are outside the spread of the fan; and at last, twenty yards up the hill your lines have converged to a point—a single foot from that point you cannot find any gold. Your breath comes short and quick, you are feverish with excitement; the dinner bell may ring its clapper off, you pay no attention; friends may die, weddings transpire, houses burn down, they are nothing to you; you sweat and dig and delve with a frantic interest—and all at once you strike it! [*Roughing It.*]

Think how much excitement Twain could have avoided by leaving out emotions and specific description of one person's actions, imaginings, dreams, even breath. Yes, but then he would have left us out too.

Certainly he would have been more dignified. More ponderous. More above-it-all. We might have thought he himself had never flushed with greed, or panned for gold. How human to admit he felt—and did—it himself. And how much easier to follow! Our main source of information, naturally, is not books, or computer printouts; it remains our own experience. We make broad generalizations on the basis of our own limited life. So why not admit it?

Here, for instance, is a writer who got stuck in the middle of his report, and confessed:

> I've stopped in mid-sentence. I'm starting off this long section: and I realize that exactly what I need at this point is a clear and concise summary statement of precisely what it is I'm going to say. And with that realization comes a trickier one: I cannot say clearly and concisely what it all amounts to. [Peter Elbow, *Writing Without Teachers.*]

What a relief! A writer who does not always stay impersonal; he even has flaws. And he admits that *he* is the person writing!

NOT SO SIMPLE AND DIRECT

Rewrite the following paragraph by Jacques Barzun substituting *I* for *it* wherever you can, making whatever other changes you need to. (Notice that for Barzun, a person does not talk; style does.)

> The best tone is the tone called plain, unaffected, unadorned. It does not talk down or jazz up; it assumes the equality of all readers likely to approach the given subject; it informs or argues without apologizing for its task; it does not try to dazzle or cajole the indifferent; it takes no posture of coziness or sophistication. [*Simple and Direct*.]

When you write about what a person does, ask yourself if there is some way you can put that person in, even if it is you. You may have some good reasons for omitting the person: you want to focus on the idea, on the action, on the general way things go. But if you make the text too empty of people, your reader may blank out. If I can't see someone doing something, I have a hard time imagining it, and after a while I altogether forget what it is. Result: you've lost me.

How about this?

> All people of broad, strong sense have an instinctive repugnance to the men of maxims; because such people early discern that the mysterious complexity of our life is not to be embraced by maxims, and that to lace ourselves up in formulas of that sort is to repress all the divine promptings and inspiration that spring from growing insight and sympathy. And the man of maxims is the popular representative of the minds that are guided in their moral judgment solely by general rules, thinking that these will lead them to justice by a ready-made patent method, without the trouble of exerting patience, discrimination, impartiality—without any care to assure themselves whether they have the insight that comes from a hardly earned estimate of temptation, or from a life vivid and intense enough to have created a wide fellow-feeling with all that is human. [George Eliot, *The Mill on the Floss*.]

By writing about mankind, rather than you and me and her, the author has made her point seem complicated, when in fact it is fairly simple. George Eliot sounds important, even thoughtful. But she has disguised her point; in fact, she has let herself get away with fairly shallow ideas, simply by talking about "people," not individuals.

So when you find yourself writing a few pages without mentioning anyone by name, or saying what someone did, or using *he,* or *she,* or *I,* or *you,* pause to ask yourself: what am I avoiding? The answer may be: people. More: taking a clear position.

Here is Abe Lincoln warning of civil war to come:

> If we could first know *where* we are, and *whither* we are tending, we could better judge *what* to do, and *how* to do it. We are now far into the fifth year, since a policy was initiated, with the *avowed* object, and confident promise, of putting an end to slavery agitation. Under the operation of that policy, that agitation has not only, *not ceased,* but has *constantly augmented.* In *my* opinion, it *will* not cease, until a *crisis* shall have been reached, and passed. A house divided against itself cannot stand. I believe this government cannot endure, permanently half *slave* and half *free.* I do not expect the Union to be *dissolved*—I do not expect the house to *fall*—but I *do* expect it will cease to be divided. It will become *all* one thing, or *all* the other.

Saying *I* helped define his position: if slavery was not stopped soon, it would spread to the whole country.

So when I get personal, I can make clear:
- My relationship to you, as one person talking to another.
- My emotional stance.
- My ideas.
- The "feel" of the acts I describe.
- The social relationships involved.

Getting personal seems friendly to me, too, because it takes away some of a writer's natural authority. And it gives us what most of us like to hear about:
- You and me.
- Him and her.
- Family ties.
- Social relationships.
- What one person (not "everyone") thought, did, and said.

In brief, to sound more human, sound like yourself—not a machine. Admit anger. Be subjective when it counts.

GETTING PERSONAL

HE could easily solve the problems of the surveyor, but he was daily beset with graver questions, which he manfully confronted. He interrogated every custom, and wished to settle all his practice on an ideal foundation. He was a protestant *à outrance,* and few lives contain so many renunciations. He was bred to no profession; he never married; he lived alone; he never went to church; he never voted; he refused to pay a tax to the state; he ate no flesh; he drank no wine, he never knew the use of tobacco; and, though a naturalist, he used neither trap nor gun. He chose, wisely no doubt for himself, to be the bachelor of thought and Nature. He had no talent for wealth, and knew how to be poor without the least hint of squalor or inelegance. Perhaps he fell into his way of living without forecasting it much, but approved it with later wisdom. "I am often reminded," he wrote in his journal, "that if I had bestowed on me the wealth of Croesus, my aims must be still the same, and my means essentially the same." He had no temptations to fight against—no appetites, no passions, no taste for elegant trifles. A fine house, dress, the manners and talk of highly cultivated people were all thrown away on him. He much preferred a good Indian, and considered these refinements as impediments to conversation, wishing to meet his companion on the simplest terms. He declined invitations to dinner-parties, because there each was in everyone's way, and he could not meet the individuals to any purpose. "They make their pride," he said, "in making their dinner cost much; I make my pride in making my dinner cost little." When asked at table what dish he preferred, he answered, "The nearest." He did not like the taste of wine, and never had a vice in his life. He said, "I have a faint recollection of pleasure derived from smoking dried lily-stems, before I was a man. I had commonly a supply of these. I have never smoked anything more noxious." [Ralph Waldo Emerson, "Thoreau."]

WHEN I was a small boy at the beginning of the century I remember an old man who wore knee-breeches and worsted stockings, and who used to hobble about the street of our village with the help of a stick. He must have been getting on for eighty in the year 1807, earlier than which date I suppose I can hardly remember him, for I was born in 1802. A few white locks hung about his ears, his shoulders were bent and his knees feeble, but he was still hale, and was much respected in our little world of Paleham. His name was Pontifex.

His wife was said to be his master; I have been told she brought him a little money, but it cannot have been much. She was a tall, square-shouldered person (I have heard my father call her a Gothic woman) who had insisted on being married to Mr. Pontifex when he was young and too good-natured to say nay to any woman who wooed him. The pair had lived not unhappily together, for Mr. Pontifex's temper was easy and he soon learned to bow before his wife's more stormy moods.

Mr. Pontifex was a carpenter by trade; he was also at one time parish clerk; when I remember him, however, he had so far risen in life as to be no longer compelled to work with his own hands. In his earlier days he had taught himself to draw. I do not say he drew well, but it was surprising he should draw as well as he did. My father, who took the living of Paleham about the year 1797, became possessed of a good many of old Mr. Pontifex's drawings, which were always of local subjects, and so unaffectedly painstaking that they might have passed for the work of some good early master. I remember them as hanging up framed and glazed in the study at the Rectory, and tinted, as else in the room was tinted, with the green reflected from the fringe of ivy leaves that grew around the windows. [Samuel Butler, *The Way of All Flesh.*]

SHE grinned and leaned and gave me a quick kiss, a quick pat, and went swiftly to the door, hauled it open, and disappeared into the busy corridor. As the door slowly, slowly closed, I had a diminishing view of an old man with a walker going along the corridor. His head was canted way over so that his cheek was almost against his left shoulder. He would slide his left foot six inches forward and then lean forward, hands braced on the aluminum tubing of the walker until his weight was over the forward foot. Then he would lift his right shoulder and turn his body to slide and swing the right foot up even with the left. He would then shove the walker another six inches forward. I had watched him in the hallway. He had all the blind, dogged, stubborn determination of a half-smashed bug heading for the darkness under the sink. It was impossible to imagine what was going on inside his skull. The door snicked shut. I wondered how many Marians the old, old man had known. I wondered if he thought of any of them, or one of them, as he made his timeless journeys, each as valiant perhaps as the last five miles of the Boston Marathon. [John D. MacDonald, *The Turquoise Lament.*]

12th DAY

Being Conversational

When we speak, our voice conveys more than the words; we say things with our gestures, our pauses, the ironic twist we put on a phrase. But when we write, we have to say it just with words.

If we wrote down what we say out loud, our readers would wonder what we meant. The thought stops in midstream. Sentences start out in one direction, end up half a block away, with the second part of one sentence becoming the beginning of the next. Incomplete sentences. Lots of repetitions. Questions and answers and exclamations. O God, conversation's a mess.

But talking is so familiar that when writing *resembles* it, we feel at ease. We imagine we hear someone talking. We are not in a book; we are in a conversation. I don't recommend transcribing exactly what you say in conversation—though that's a good way to figure out what you think. I do recommend letting yourself use some of the conventions of ordinary speech. Why? It's more relaxed: lets the reader take off his shoes, get comfortable: lets you do that too. It reads like a real person talking. It puts you on the same level as the reader—not above.

First, I admit there are times when you ought not to sound like just folks chatting. For instance, if you're announcing the formation of a new country, you'll want to issue a declaration that sounds like quill pens scratching on sheepskin:

> When, in the course of human events, it becomes necessary for one people to dissolve the political bands which have connected them with another, and to assume among the powers of the earth the separate and equal station to which the laws of nature and of nature's God entitle them, a decent respect to the opinions of mankind requires that they should declare the causes which impel them to the separation. [Thomas Jefferson, *Declaration of Independence.*]

Quite appropriate, Mr. Jefferson. But that style does not really suit business letters, or essays, or proposals, or reports, or even magazine articles—or most of what we write. And in those areas, we *do* tend to be a little stuffy—the result of years of training to use big words, to sound grown-up when we weren't. And now that we are, many of us go on talking big. That's why I say: relax.

Developing a conversational style of writing requires that you let go of a number of rules you learned were absolutes. Not abandoning them. Just spotting times when you can let them drop for a moment. For instance, incomplete sentences.

Here's a sample of real speech, edited by Studs Terkel, when he was tape-recording people for one of his books:

> "When people ask you what you're doing and you say stewardess, you're really proud, you think it's great. It's like a stepping stone. The first two months I started flying I had already been to London, Paris, and Rome. And me from Broken Bow, Nebraska. But after you start working, it's not as glamorous as you thought it was going to be." [*Working.*]

"And me from Broken Bow, Nebraska." It ain't proper, but it's the way we talk. Her point is clear, even in an incomplete sentence. We should write in units that are complete thoughts, sure; but that does not *always* mean those units have to be "complete sentences."

GRAMMAR SCHOOL EXERCISE

Remember someone who taught you grammar, and describe that person using both complete and incomplete sentences. What was your main impression of that person?

_____

_____

_____

In excited conversation, we may hem and haw, strike out in one direction, stop, head some other way: but we are always struggling toward a point. That feeling of driving forward to an idea we have not yet quite been able to express, can make your written paragraphs sound more like speech. Here, for instance, is a free-lance private eye, name of McGee:

> I had believed her empathetic, sensitive, responsive. I had enjoyed being with her. This female person did not seem at all responsive in the same way. I went back over the relationship. A cartoon light bulb went on in the air over my head. At all prior times, up to last night and now, my involvement had been in exactly the same track as her self-involvement. So of course she had been responsive, in the way a mirror is responsive.
>
> If you go to a play which is concerned with a dramatic relationship you have experienced, you are deeply moved. The actress will speak the lines in a way best designed to move you. But take the lovely, talented thing to dinner, and she will bury you in the debris of her tepid little mind, rotten reviews in London, the inferior dressing room on the Coast, the pansy hairdresser's revenge, her manager's idiot wife, the trouble with talk shows, and who has stopped or started sleeping with whom or with what.
>
> I had listened to drama and believed it. And now I could not believe that this was the actress. [John D. MacDonald, *The Scarlet Ruse.*]

When your writing acquires that almost conversational struggle toward expression, we too search, we ponder possibilities. Our minds help you reach your goal.

VEERING AND TACKING

Describe how you went about finding some place you had forgotten, or never known. How did you get past the feeling that you were lost? Take us through the thoughts you had, as you looked here and there, and then here again. And how did it feel to find that place at last? (Feel free to use exclamation points, contractions like *I'd*, and incomplete sentences):

_____

_____

_____

_____

The more you put in quotes, the more popular your work will be. (Popular fiction, for instance, is often more than 50 percent dialogue.) If you listen to someone else's conversation, particularly when they are caught up in what they are saying, you will find they are quoting someone else, then quoting their own response, and so on. When we talk, we often repeat conversations we've just had—with comments. So try that when you write.

Direct quotations, then—not a digest of what someone said. The exact words. In quotation marks. And if you said something back, all the better: put that in too.

And if you feel like it, talk directly to the reader. Let the reader join your kaffeeklatsch.

RECALLING

Recall a conversation that bothered you in the last day or so. Or, even better, spy on someone else's conversation at lunch or in public. Get the exact words said, on both sides.

_____

_____

_____

_____

_____

_____

By suggesting that the reader has joined a conversation that has several voices, you avoid lecturing. And you can awaken even more interest if the conversation becomes a quarrel. With a fight, we want to know who's going to win; we choose sides; we think more. If you quote both sides, you can ask the reader who he agrees with.

MANAGING AN ARGUMENT

Quote someone you've read in this book, then argue with them. Try to limit the quotations to a sentence or so, and make your responses snappy.

_____

_____

_____

_____

_____

_____

_____

_____

_____

_____

_____

Dialogue arouses more interest than general conclusions do.

MEANINGFUL EXERCISE

Think of someone whose views you have to listen to, but don't like. Quote that person as accurately as you can, then respond with what you'd _like_ to say out loud, if you could. Work to a crescendo.

_____

_____

_____

_____

_____

_____

_____

_____

_____

But, there is the danger of sounding too much like real talk. For instance, you might end up drivelling like this geezer Mark Twain found in one of the mining towns:

"Rev. Leonidas W. . . . H'm, Reverend Le—well, there was a feller here once by the name of *Jim* Smiley, in the winter of '49, or maybe it was the spring of '50—I don't recollect exactly, somehow, though, what makes me think it was one or the other is because I remember the big flume warn't finished when he first came to the camp; but anyway. . . . ["Notorious Jumping Frog of Calaveras County."]

Even Twain ran away from that guy.

Or you may repeat yourself too much. That's easy to fix when you go back and edit. But it happens. Also, you may lose your tone of authority. You may not sound so much like an expert. (If that is your pay ticket, then go back to the unpronounceable jargon and the three-paragraph sentences.)

But the more you play with writing *as if* you were actually talking, the more you'll find you can drive on through the evidence and the quotes and the arguing; you can come out on the other side, with an idea fully developed in your hand. Out loud we have rhythm: get some of that onto the page.

Some techniques we've talked about in other chapters can help, too: for instance, when we speak, we tend to use parallel form to emphasize that something happens over and over. We get very specific about prices and locations. We mention lots of people, and describe them in very personal terms.

Loosening up your writing lets your feelings show through, too. Here, for instance, is John Steinbeck writing about the ruined harvests in *The Grapes of Wrath:* "And first the cherries ripen. Cent and a half a pound. Hell, we can't pick 'em for that. Black cherries and red cherries, full and sweet, and the birds eat half of each cherry and the yellowjackets buzz into the holes the birds made."

And George Eliot, on farming:

As for farming, it's putting money into your pocket wi' your right hand and fetching it out wi' your left. As fur as I can see, it's raising victual for other folks, and just getting a mouthful for yourself and your children as you go along. . . . It's more than flesh and blood 'ull bear sometimes, to be toiling and striving and up early and down late, and hardly sleeping a wink when you lie down for thinking as the cheese may swell, or the cows may slip their calf, or the wheat may grow green again i' the sheaf—and after all, at th' end of the year, it's like as if you'd been cooking a feast and had got the smell of it for your pains. [*Adam Bede.*]

Of course, it's risky to loosen up like that. But remember the benefits:
- You sound like a real person.
- You let the reader relax.
- Your emotions show through faster.
- You draw readers along as you push toward your point.

So, when you think you can risk sounding as if you're actually talking to a reader, let yourself:
- Ask questions—and answer them.
- Talk directly to the reader.
- Use exclamation marks!
- Leave some sentences incomplete.
- Quote, quote, quote.
- Argue out loud.

MORE QUOTES WITH A CONVERSATIONAL TONE

J UST a minute," says Benny Bentley as the phone rings. "Let me take this call, then I got something to show you. Just hold on." He picks up the phone. "Hello. Yeah, this is Bentley. I got no tickets at all, not a one. But wait a minute, for you I think I can scare up a couple. That's all right, don't thank me; the tickets'll be in your name at the box office." Bentley hangs up. "My tax accountant," he says. "How can I say no to him? He screws up one figure and I end up in jail."

Bentley is in the headquarters of the Chicago Bulls. He has been the Bulls' Publicity and Public Relations Director for the past six years, and of course he is good at it. Benny Bentley can hustle anything; he has done it for most of his 50 years, and a successful NBA club is no trick at all for him. But somehow, swiveling in his chair in the Bulls' offices at the Sheraton-Chicago, Bentley does not look right. After all these years, he is still a boxing man, and he does not fit in here.

"Yeah, but how can you fight it anymore?" Bentley says. "Who do you have trying to run boxing? A bunch of guys who talk about image and ask you to write them out proposals. *Proposals!* A real fight man never wrote out a proposal in his life. Think about Al Weill. This man was not the best-liked human being ever to walk the earth, but he had a shrewdness in him you couldn't get at Yale or Harvard. You can't show me a Yale man who could take a crude kid like Marciano and make him the heavyweight champion of the whole world. A man like Weill, he could tear your heart out for two and a half per cent. That's what you need in boxing, that kind of mind, not some guy in a button-down suit who's going to ask you for a *proposal,* for chrissake." [Bob Greene, *Johnny Deadline, Reporter.*]

W HEN I was sixteen, I went wrong. I'm upwards of thirty now. I've been fourteen or fifteen years at it. It's one of those things you can't well leave off when you've once took to it. I was born in Chatham. We had a small baker's shop there, and I served customers and minded the shop. There's lots of soldiers at Chatham, as you know, and they used to look in at the window in passing, and nod and laugh whenever they could catch my eye. I liked to be noticed by the soldiers. At last one young fellow, a recruit, who had not long joined, I think, for he told me he hadn't been long at the depot, came in and talked to me. Well, this went on, and things fell out as they always do with girls who go about with men, more especially soldiers, and when the regiment went to Ireland, he gave me a little money that helped me to follow it; and I went about from place to place, time after time, always sticking to the same regiment. My first man got tired of me in a year or two, but that didn't matter. I took up with a sergeant then, which was a cut above a private, and helped me on wonderful. When we were at Dover, there was a militia permanently embodied artillery regiment quartered with us on the western heights, and I got talking to some of the officers, who liked me a bit. I was a damn sight prettier then than I am now, you may take your dying oath, and they noticed me uncommon: and although I didn't altogether cut my old friends, I carried on with these fellows all the time we were there, and made a lot of money, and bought better dresses, and some jewelry, that altered me wonderfully. . . .

. . . I don't get much—very little, hardly enough to live upon. I've done a little needlework in the daytime. I don't now, although I do some washing and mangling now and then to help it out. I don't pay much for my bed-room, only six bob a week, and dear at that. It ain't much of a place. Some of the girls about here live in houses. I don't; I never could abear it. You ain't your own master, and I always liked my freedom. I'm not comfortable, exactly; it's a brutal sort of life this. It isn't the sin of it, though, that worries me. I don't dare think of that much, but I do think how happy I might have been if I'd always lived at Chatham, and married as other women do, and had a nice home and children; that's what I want, and when I think of all that, I do cut up.   [Henry Mayhew, *London Labour and the London Poor.*]

AT thirty-two I was seeking a change of pace. I took some time to look at myself and grow, and decided to apply at several graduate schools to gain a doctoral degree in psychology.

I wasn't accepted then. One school said I was too old and probably too set in my mind to learn anything new. They also felt I might be too rigid because I was a minister. I accepted a call to Grace Lutheran Church in Richmond, California. I was able to shift down some. I was still in conflict between wanting to be a psychologist or remaining in the parish ministry. My blood pressure began to climb, and the physician warned me that if I didn't slow down, I could have a coronary in ten years. So again I decided to apply for graduate school. I was finally accepted into a graduate department of psychology. I worked hard and fast to get through school before the money ran out. I went to school year-round and spent two years as an intern psychologist at the state hospital part time. I completed a four-year program in two years, but I deluded myself into believing I wasn't falling back into my workaholic lifestyle. I thought I was learning to say no and not feel guilty, but I was only kidding myself. [Ken Olson, *Hey Man, Open Up and Live!*]

13th DAY

Breaking In

When we talk, we often break into our own sentences to add extra information, or simply to emphasize. We stop for a moment to heighten the drama, then—by isolating it from the rest of what we say—we stress what comes next.

In writing, we have punctuation marks to suggest these pauses. A period makes a full stop. A colon: slightly less. A semicolon, still less; a comma, even shorter. The two marks used most to indicate that you are butting into your own sentences are the parenthesis (a quiet aside, slightly more than a comma), and the dash—a dramatic flourish.

We'll concentrate on the dash. (The parenthesis is so much less important. It qualifies, adds nonessential information, apologizes for itself. Parentheses are shy inserts). A dash can make your writing sound more casual. For instance, when Charles Lamb began glorifying roast pig by devoting a whole "dissertation" to it, he made his essay sound like an after-dinner speech—full of mock serious comments and jokes:

> I speak not of your grown porkers—things between pig and pork—those hobbydehoys—but a young and tender suckling—under a moon old—guiltless as yet of the sty—with no original speck of the *amor immunditiae,* the hereditary failing of the first parent, yet manifest—his voice as yet not broken, but something between a childish treble and a grumble—the mild forerunner, or praeludium of a grunt. . . . Pig—let me speak his praise! ["Dissertation on a Roast Pig."]

Dashes also make writing sound as if you are thinking as you go—qualifying, expanding, running on pell-mell. In fact, using a lot of dashes can make your writing rush on like a letter. Some people think dashes look illiterate. Perhaps they do—if overdone.

MAD EXERCISE

Describe a mad dash you've made—on foot or not. Throw in lots of dashes. Make the rhythm of the writing imitate the speeds (and, perhaps, the brief stalls) you describe.

_____

_____

_____

_____

_____

_____

ADDING A DASH

Here is a description of buffalo hunting by Francis Parkman. Insert dashes wherever you can, and contemplate the difference they make in the pace.

> The chief difficulty in running buffalo . . . is that of loading the gun or pistol at full gallop. Many hunters for convenience's sake carry three or four bullets in the mouth; the powder is poured down the muzzle of the piece, the bullet dropped in after it, the stock struck hard upon the pommel of the saddle, and the work is done. The danger of this is obvious. Should the blow on the pommel fail to send the bullet home, or should the bullet, in the act of aiming, start from its place and roll toward the muzzle, the gun would probably burst in discharging. Many a shattered hand and worse casualties besides have been the result of such an accident. [*The California and Oregon Trail.*]

A dash then, acts as a rhythmic accent. It stresses—and isolates—what comes next. Done often enough, it can make us breathless. But used with restraint, the dash can do more than loosen up the sound of your writing. It can emphasize, too.

When Stephen Crane wrote of abandoning ship, he said that he felt friendly toward the other men in his lifeboat. But *friends* did not seem to say enough, so he added a dash, and explained how much more than ordinary friendliness this was. Notice how the dash functions as a pivot, turning the mind from ordinary to extraordinary comradeship:

> It would be difficult to describe the subtle brotherhood of men that was here established on the seas. No one said that it was so. No one mentioned it. But it dwelt in the boat, and each man felt it warm him. They were a captain, an oiler, a cook, and a correspondent, and they were friends—friends in a more curiously iron-bound degree than may be common. The hurt captain, lying against the water jar in the bow, spoke always in a low voice and calmly; but he could never command a more ready and swiftly obedient crew than the motley three of the dinghy. It was more than a mere recognition of what was best for the common safety. There was surely in it a quality that was personal and heart-felt. And after this devotion to the commander of the boat, there was this comradeship, that the correspondent, for instance, who had been taught to be cynical of men, knew even at the time was the best experience of his life. But no one said that it was so. No one mentioned it. [*The Open Boat.*]

Similarly, Lewis Mumford resorts to a dash for one extra dollop of proof—extra, but crucial. He has been suggesting that mechanical clocks may have originated in medieval monasteries, because the monks—particularly the Benedictines—worked set hours, marked by regular bells. Mumford cannot prove that the monks brought clocks, and with them, a collective schedule, to the culture, but he thinks so, and his strongest proof is that there were so many monasteries in that period of shallow population.

> So one is not straining the facts when one suggests that the monasteries—at one time there were 40,000 under the Benedictine rule—helped give human enterprise the regular collective beat and rhythm of the machine; for the clock is not merely a means of keeping track of the hours, but of synchronizing the actions of men. [*Technics and Civilization.*]

After a long list, or a complicated sentence, a dash can separate your point from the chaff. For instance, the historian Macaulay wanted to point out that in the battle of Landen the commanders were so poor and sickly—one a hunchbacked dwarf and the other an asthmatic skeleton—that in any other period, they would have been left behind. So he began by listing physically powerful warriors from earlier eras:

> Ajax beating down the Trojan leader with a rock which two ordinary men could scarcely lift, Horatius defending the bridge against an army, Richard the Lion-Hearted spurring along the whole Saracen line without finding an enemy to withstand his assault, Robert Bruce crushing with one blow the helmet and head of Sir Henry Bohun in sight of the whole array of England and Scotland—such are the heroes of a dark age. [*History of England.*]

Or take e.e. cummings, describing the way he and his fellow prisoners made up a notebook full of colors. For them, this was art. But for most Americans, he feels, this would not be art, because Americans have one drawback: "The Great American Public has a handicap which my friends at La Ferte did not as a rule have—education."

By setting *education* off at the end, distinguished by a dash, cummings makes the word snap. He means to slap us with that idea. So whenever you find your paragraphs rambling on, or falling into mere lists, draw up short—and make your point with a dash.

A caution: if you insert a phrase and dashes between your subject and your verb, the reader may forget the sentence. Don't get between words that naturally go together.

Throwing in a dash or two, then, can break up a monotonous rhythm, making your writing sound more casual (more like speech or an informal letter). One dash acts as a theatrical hesitation; many dashes suggest hectic speed—thinking as you write. And a judiciously placed dash can help the sense, as well as the sound, by setting off your main idea.

Open up your prose. These devices (the parentheses, the dash, even commas) let air and light into your writing. An occasional short paragraph or sentence can do that too. Of course, the fastest way to lighten your prose is the easiest: use more white space.

DOTS AND DASHES

EVERY neck is stretched further, and every eye strained wider. Away across the endless dead level of the prairie a black speck appears against the sky, and it is plain that it moves. Well, I should think so! In a second or two, it becomes a horse and rider, rising and falling, rising and falling—sweeping toward us nearer and nearer—growing more and more distinct, more and more sharply defined—nearer and still nearer, and the flutter of the hoofs comes faintly to the ear—another instant a whoop and a hurrah from our upper deck, a wave of the rider's hand, but no reply, and man and horse burst past our excited faces, and go winging away like a belated fragment of a storm! [Mark Twain, *Roughing It.*]

I DO not know how it is with others, but I feel the better always for the perusal of one of Congreve's—nay, why should I not add, even of Wycherly's—comedies. I am the gayer at least for it; and I could never connect those sports of a witty fancy in any shape with any result to be drawn from them to imitation in real life. They are a world of themselves almost as much as fairyland. [Charles Lamb, On the Artificial Comedy of the Last Century.]

THE Cumberland was on a regular bender. We passed several small villages, completely inundated; some of the houses floating off and others stationary with nothing but the chimneys visible.

In the villages built higher up on the bluffs, everything appeared like a Sunday; no smoke visible, except from an occasional chimney—no doors open—no signs of life—no citizens except occasionally a solitary butternut as the soldiers called them. One instance I recollect, where we must have sailed through the door yard of a cabin (if cabins have such things in Dixie), the inmates were assembled on the rude porch, five dirty children, three dirty, tangle-haired, parchment-faced women, sans crinoline, sans shoes, sans stockings—half a dozen dogs of low degree, and one middle-aged, lantern-jawed long-haired butternut-clad concern such as they called a man in Dixie. [Major Connolly, "Letters to His Wife."]

14th DAY

Simplifying

The more profound the idea, the simpler its expression. "Out of the mouths of babes . . ."

When you make writing complex, you seem to add meaning, but in fact each extra phrase tends to limit the subject, narrow the application, modify and qualify.

Fancy phrases make us look at the language, not the thought. Twists and tangles draw us off the main path, lose us in the jungle. Heavyweight words may stun us, like bombs, but they rarely say much.

When Maxim Gorki read the first draft of his play about bums and whores to Leo Tolstoy, the novelist complained, ". . . your language is very skillful, with all kinds of tricks—that's no good. You ought to write more simply; people speak simply, even incoherently, and that's good. A peasant doesn't ask: 'Why is a third more than a fourth, if four is always more than three,' as one learned young lady asked. No tricks, please." [Maxim Gorky, *Reminiscences of Tolstoy, Chekov, & Andreev.*]

Simple writing says more faster, in less words. For instance, the reader does not have to waste time figuring out what you mean; as a result, he does not resist you because of your style, and he may have some energy left to think about what you are saying. But then, to produce that effect, *you* may have to work harder.

When we first learn some literary tricks, we may rely on them too much, hoping to impress our readers. Simplifying takes more effort; forces us to know what we mean to say; grants the reader a chance to understand, and disagree. Simplifying does not mean cutting out important ideas, or what they imply. It does not mean writing down—a form of snobbery. The hard part of simplifying is this: to express everything you want to, and cut out everything else.

To talk fully, but simply, we have to start by looking at the reasons we may tend to get tricky. We may be lazy: when pressed for time, it's always easier to write a longer, less coherent paper. We may want to show off. We may be nervous at having so little to say. We may just be carried away by wild-eyed notions, babbling. Or we may not want to seem blunt, crude, or common.

Here, for instance, is the way philosopher Walter Kaufmann explained fondness for using difficult, specialized jargon by saying, "Men love jargon. It is so palpable, tangible, visible, audible; it makes so obvious what one has learned; it satisfies the craving for results. It is impressive for the uninitiated. It makes one feel that one belongs. Jargon divides men into Us and Them."

So cut down on jargon, when you can. But more important, notice the impulse. When you feel that impulse, alarms should go off, alerting you that you are about to go gaga with big-gun words. Jargon's not all bad: you just don't need it that often. You need it when you are telling another expert in your field something so precise that if you didn't use jargon, he'd be uncertain as to what you mean. Otherwise, forget it.

JABBERWOCKY

First, let's abuse our own jargon for a while. Think of some field you know well: at home, or at work. Then write a few sentences that would baffle an outsider, someone not in the know. Underneath, translate that into one simple sentence.

_____

_____

_____

_____

Translation: _____

Similar impulses may lead us to use five words where one would do. What could make you write "In the event that," when you mean "If"? Cut out the padding.

INSTEAD OF ...	WRITE ...
Due to the fact that	Because
For a period of a week	For one week
Disappear from view	Disappear
Appear on the scene	Appear
At this present point in time	Now
A total of ten	Ten
Until such time as	Until
I am of the opinion that	I think

Sometimes we write in pairs (each and every, part and parcel, betwixt and between, really and truly, separate and distinct). Instead, pick one. Also, tame the intensifiers: do you really need to say _really, absolutely,_ and _entirely_? Omit extra words.

DIETING

Reduce the phrase on the left to one word.

Concerning the matter of   _____

With regard to   _____

In respect to the matter of   _____

Absolutely nothing   _____

Circle around   _____

Really and truly   _____

Shuttle back and forth   _____

Ways and means   _____

Extra clauses sprout from bad prose, drawing our attention away from the main subject and its verb. If you hear *that*'s and *which*'s clattering in your prose, turn some of those clauses into adjectives or separate sentences. Remember James Thurber's famous warning about which-whiching: "It is well to remember that one 'which' leads to two and that two 'whiches' multiply like rabbits. You should never start out with the idea that you can get by with one 'which.' Suddenly they are all around you."

AXING CLAUSES

Condense these sentences. Get rid of the *that* and *which* and *who* clauses by reducing them to a word, or by starting a new sentence.

1. The idea that I thought of at that moment in time, which was nearly noon, was that I might like to eat a meal, which would be lunch. _____

_____

2. It seems to this writer that, in the case of these students, who are rated very low on each and every intelligence test, which the writer admits may not be an absolutely certain way of measuring their skill, this university, which needs all the tuition income it can get, should not turn away people who can afford to pay. _____

_____

Short sentences make sense. They give us a break when they show up in the middle of a string of longer ones. We can see the idea. And we can tell if it adds anything to what has gone before. Here, for instance, is Jack London reporting on what San Francisco looked like after the 1906 earthquake for *Collier's*. As he walks through the damaged city, waiting for the firestorm to hit, each sentence records a new impression:

> At nine o'clock Wednesday evening I walked down through the very heart of the city. I walked through miles and miles of magnificent buildings and towering skyscrapers. Here was no fire. All was in perfect order. The police patrolled the streets. Every building had its watchman at the door. And yet it was doomed, all of it. There was no water. The dynamite was giving out. And at right angles two different conflagrations were sweeping down upon it.
> At one o'clock in the morning I walked down through the same section. Everything still stood intact. There was no fire. And yet there was a change. A

rain of ashes was falling. The watchmen at the doors were gone. The police had been withdrawn. There were no firemen, no fire engines, no men fighting with dynamite. The district had been absolutely abandoned. I stood at the corner of Kearney and Market, in the very innermost heart of San Francisco. Kearney Street was deserted. Half a dozen blocks away it was burning on both sides. The street was a wall of flame, and against this wall of flame, silhouetted sharply, were two U.S. cavalrymen sitting on their horses, calmly watching. That was all. Not another person was in sight. In the intact heart of the city two troopers sat their horses and watched.

SHORTENING UP

Amateurs overwrite; professional writers tend to trim. Rewrite each of the following sentences so that you preserve the gist of it while using fewer words:
1. The writer must earn money in order to be able to live and to write, but he must by no means live and write for the purpose of making money. [Karl Marx.]

_____

_____

2. Find out just what people will submit to, and you have found out the exact amount of injustice and wrong which will be imposed upon them, and these will continue till they have resisted with either words or blows, or with both. [Frederick Douglass.] _____

_____

3. Our press law is such that divergencies of opinion between members of the government are no longer an occasion for public exhibitions, which are not the newspaper's business. [Adolf Hitler.] _____

_____

4. I will say nothing against the course of my existence, but at bottom it has been nothing but pain and burden, and I can affirm that during the whole of my seventy-five years, I have not had four weeks of genuine well-being. [Johann Wolfgang von Goethe.] _____

_____

In school and business, we're trained to patch noun to noun, and talk in clumps; designed to avoid saying anything, these phrases suggest meanings, but never spell them out. The Royal Canadian Air Force made up a list of fuzzy phrases, and Philip Broughton, who works for the U.S. Public Health Service, drew up his Systematic Buzz Phrase Projector, so bureaucrats could sound good without saying anything. Here is a similar "system." Just take one word from A, one from B, and one from C:

A	B	C
non-functional	displacement	research
disparate	encounter-type	relationship

emergency	self-reflexive	capability
community-based	inter-branch	analysis
optimal	non-conventional	contingency
interconnected	multi-input	triage
real-time	time-shared	interface

Even if you don't write throat-chokers like that, you may still be using bigger words than you need to. Most add syllables without adding to or refining the meaning. Why do we reach for them, then? The tone, usually: like children, we associate big words with authority, serious purpose, and expertise. But big words also help us avoid realizing what we mean. For instance, when we first heard of *limited-duration protective-reaction retaliatory strikes* it sounded as if we were doing something (just what was not clear) that would not last very long, but that would strike back at someone in order to protect ourselves. Only gradually did we find out that the Pentagon was talking about large-scale bombing.

THINK

What one-syllable word could you put in place of the one on the left?

Abode _____

Commence _____

Commandment _____

Gender _____

Liquid refreshment _____

Optimal _____

Residence _____

Utilize _____

Verbalize _____

Of course, sometimes you must use complicated language. But not too often. Unless you make your living by lying, you can afford plain talk.

Remember, simplifying means reducing what you want to say to the simplest form. It does not mean throwing away key ideas; just boiling them down to their essence. It does not mean sacrificing your dignity. But simplifying does mean you have to work hard to condense so that the reader does not have to work so hard to decipher. Being simple, then, is just another way of being friendly.

So, to write simply,

- Stay alert for impulses to get complicated.
- Avoid jargon.
- Omit needless words.
- Cut out subordinate clauses.
- Make sentences brief.
- Use short words.

STRAIGHT AND SIMPLE

I ALWAYS write my letters post-haste, and so rashly headlong that even when I write intolerably badly, I would rather write with my own hand than employ another: for I find no one can imitate me, and I never copy them over again. I have accustomed those great people who know me to endure blots, blurs, dashes, and botches in my letters, and a sheet without folding or margin. Those letters that have cost me the most labor or research are the worst. When I once begin to ramble, it is a sign my mind is not on them. I commonly begin without an outline: the first word begets the second. [Michel de Montaigne, "Considering Cicero."]

AN author can hardly hope to be popular unless he can use popular language. That is quite true; but then comes the question of achieving a popular—in other words, I may say, a good and lucid style. How may an author best acquire a mode of writing which shall be agreeable and easily intelligible to the reader?... His language must come from him as music comes from the rapid touch of the great performer's fingers; as words come from the mouth of an indignant orator; as letters fly from the fingers of the trained compositor; as the syllables tinkled out by little bells form themselves to the ear of the telegraphist. A man who thinks much of his words as he writes them will generally leave behind him work that smells of oil. [Anthony Trollope, *Autobiography*.]

OMIT NEEDLESS WORDS. Vigorous writing is concise. A sentence should contain no unnecessary words, a paragraph no unnecessary sentences, for the same reason that a drawing should have no unnecessary lines, and a machine no unnecessary parts. This requires not that the writer make all his sentences short, or that he avoid all detail and treat his subjects only in outline, but that every word tell. [William B. Strunk, Jr., and E. B. White, *The Elements of Style*.]

15th DAY

Running Metaphors

When Mao said a guerrilla moves among the people like a fish in water, he reduced a theory of revolution to an image. We can see the picture—the fish swimming away, protected by the water, nourished by it, almost part of it. We can feel, too, the emotion of the fisherman on the bank: Oh, he got away! Then, while we hold that vision in our mind, Mao gives us ideas of what it means.

And when Jonathan Swift brooded on the poverty of eighteenth-century Ireland, he noticed thousands of children starving, begging, and stealing food. When they grew up, they would not be able to find jobs, except as thieves or whores; most would soon die, or sell themselves to foreigners as servants or soldiers. Swift thought they might as well be dead. So why not kill them? Even better, sell them as meat to the very men who had ruined Ireland: absentee English landlords. After all, these landlords were already, in effect, killing the children for the sake of profits, skinning them alive, treating them like—or worse than—cattle. That picture of selling children as meat became the central image around which he organized his attack on the wealthy Englishmen. Of course, he admits the costs: "I grant this food will be somewhat dear, and therefore very proper for landlords, who, as they have already devoured most of the parents, seem to have the best title to the children." [*A Modest Proposal.*]

A strong image can help you organize a number of abstract ideas, while coloring them with emotion. And the reader can make sense of what you say, by connecting each new thought with the over-all picture. Later, to recall the ideas, the reader can summon up the picture—something he looked at, in his mind, all the time you were talking theory—and from that, gradually, he can reconstruct your ideas.

For example, when the novelist Arthur Koestler began to write about his fellow authors, he sketched out this picture:

> One of the great Russians—I think it was Turgenev—could only write with his feet in a bucket of hot water under his desk, facing the open window of his room. I believe that this position is typical for the novelist. The hot water bucket stands for inspiration, the subconscious, the creative source, or whatever you like to call it. The open window stands for the world outside, the raw material for the artist's creation. [*The Yogi and the Commissar.*]

Koestler then went on to "interpret" the picture. Some writers close the shutters—ignore the real world altogether. Others get drawn outside, and lose themselves in it. Still others stay in, but adjust the shutters so they only have to look at a narrow slice of existence. Thus, the initial image helps Koestler organize his ideas about different ways writers approach—or avoid—the real world.

On the surface, then, a metaphor is anything we can see—a picture, an event, a single image—which *stands for* a number of ideas. The metaphor also tinges those ideas with the emotions it evokes and the associations it calls up. So when you decide to use an image, be clear about what it stands for, and, just as important, what it suggests.

FROM IDEAS TO IMAGES

Here are some ideas: think them over, and come up with two pictures that sum them up. To see how the image affects the emotional response, make one picture positive, the other negative.

The Ideas: Geniuses do not usually follow the rules.

Geniuses sometimes wear strange clothes.

Geniuses seem to hate conventional thought.

Geniuses have energy that does not always seem
to be under control.

Positive Image: A genius is . . . ─────────────────────────

───

Negative Image: A genius is . . . ─────────────────────────

───

You may find yourself with any number of ideas that do not easily fit together in a logical way. You feel a connection, but cannot spell it out, or number the connecting links. *That* is the time to consider using an image that you can tie each idea to—a metaphor that runs throughout your piece.

Of course, as you struggle to find that one image, you may stumble through three or four that don't fit together. For instance, a political boss once summed up the race for president this way: "It's a yo-yo situation. We've had the 2nd inning of a 38-inning ball game. Reagan did very well, but it's still a horse race." Pick one sport, and stick to it—or you'll end up with some horse batting a yo-yo in the ninth inning.

One image, then, not half a dozen. And once you have the metaphor, spell out *what* you are comparing to *what* right off. Then ask yourself: exactly how is my subject like that? The more parallels you turn up, the easier it will be for the reader to follow the connection.

For instance, after his ship sank, Stephen Crane spent several nights in a small boat in the open ocean. Trying to describe the movements the rowboat went through, he thought of a bucking bronco. Watch how many ways he draws out that comparison:

A seat in this boat was not unlike a seat upon a bucking bronco, and by the same token a bronco is not much smaller. The craft pranced and reared and plunged like an animal. As each wave came, and she rose for it, she seemed like a horse making at a fence outrageously high. The manner of her scramble over these walls of water is a mystic thing, and moreover, at the top of them were ordinarily thése problems in white water, the foam racing down from the summit of each wave requiring a new leap, and a leap from the air. Then, after scornfully bumping a crest, she would slide and race and splash down a long incline, and arriving bobbing and nodding in front of the next menace. [*The Open Boat.*]

Crane gives the boat a sex, like a horse. He says the size is the same, and he shows that both make the same moves: prancing, rearing, plunging "like an animal," rising "like a horse making at a fence," scrambling, bumping, sliding, racing, bobbing, and nodding.

When you are going to use a comparison at length, to give shape to your paragraph, be sure to use words that evoke the picture throughout.

SWIMMING

Think of watching someone swim. First, figure out what that person has in common with a whale, or a dolphin. Then, picking your best images, write a short paragraph drawing out that comparison. What moves are the same? What looks the same? What else is similar?

_____

_____

_____

_____

_____

An image can help you pin down some vague sensation, so that you can proceed to spell out exactly what suggested that image to you, as Charles Dickens does here:

As if she were a part of the refuse the city had cast out, and left to corruption and decay, the girl we had followed strayed down to the river's brink, and stood in the midst of this night-picture, lonely and still, looking at the water. . . .

I think she was talking to herself. I am sure, although absorbed in gazing at the water, that her shawl was off her shoulders, and that she was muffling her hands in it, in an unsettled and bewildered way, more like the action of a sleep-walker than a waking person. I know, and never can forget, that there was that in her wild manner which gave me no assurance but that she would sink before my eyes, until I had her arm within my grasp. . . .

We carried her away from the water to where there were some dry stones, and there laid her down, crying and moaning. In a little while she sat among the stones holding her wretched head with both her hands. "Oh, the river!" she cried passionately. "Oh, the river!" [*David Copperfield.*]

The girl had been cast off by her rich seducer. Like the trash washed down into the Thames by heavy rain, she stands there waiting to be swept away. Perhaps she imagines the great dark waters will cleanse her, or kill her, or erase her memory. One broad image, then, suggests all three meanings, without negating any one of them.

ETHNIC IMAGE

Think of an ethnic group you yourself identify with, and reach for an image that you could use if you were going to write a long paper describing them as a group. What picture seems to you to sum up their situation, their identity?

_____

_____

_____

_____

_____

And what exactly would give rise to that impression? What traits, what typical jobs, attitudes, life experiences, would lead you to sum up the group that way?

_____

_____

_____

_____

_____

_____

As a writer, you may proceed from a vague feeling to some image, and from spelling out why you thought of that to ideas that explain and give it depth. For the reader, though, that image is what she sees throughout: the ideas arise and dissolve. Later, if she recalls your writing at all, she will remember the image. And if that had some strong emotional content, she may also, gradually, with effort, resurrect some of the reasons you thought that picture a true one.

So what are the circumstances in which you may want to use a running metaphor? Whenever . . .

- You have a lot of ideas that do not easily fit together.
- You want to evoke emotional associations.
- You want a strong image to sum up your message.
- You want to be remembered.

Reach for an image: and when you do,

- Make it clear. (Can we see it?)
- Spell out what it stands for.
- Understand what emotions it arouses. (Are they appropriate?)
- Throughout, choose words that refer to both the idea and the image.

MORE METAPHORS

ONCE upon a time, the American met the automobile and fell in love. Unfortunately, this led him into matrimony, and so he did not live happily ever after. Cooler heads could have told him the affair was doomed from the start, for in the beginning, the American was poorly prepared to make judgments in such matters. He was merely a rustic Merry Andrew with a cowlick and an adolescent tightening in the groin. In his libidinous innocence, he saw the automobile only as curious, exciting—and obviously willing. Wherefore, he joyfully leaped upon her, and she responded to his caresses by bolting about the landscape in what can only be called a succession of bumps and grinds. [John Keats, *The Insolent Chariots.*]

IF one were forced to choose a single aspect of Houston and from that aspect infer or characterize the city I think I would choose its bars, or, to be fully accurate, its bars and clubs. The upper class, for the most part, inhabits the upper air. Their clubs are very posh, if in a somewhat River Okie way, and tend to be altitudinally remote. There is a club on top of almost every tall building in town; the elevation they provide is both physical and psychological. They help relieve the hunger for heights that can seize one in a city only forty-one feet above sea level; and they also put their members well above the masses who cannot afford such relief. [Larry McMurty, *In a Narrow Grave.*]

JANINE had nailed it. People hate their cars. Daddy doesn't come proudly home with the new one any more, and the family doesn't come racing out, yelling wow, and the neighbors don't come over to admire it. They all look alike, for one thing. So you have to wedge a piece of bright trash atop the aerial to find your own. They may be named after predators, or primitive emotions, or astronomical objects, but in essence they are a big, shiny sink down which the money swirls—in insurance, car payments, tags, tolls, tires, repairs. They give you a chance to sit in helpless rage, beating on the steering wheel in a blare of horns while, a mile away, your flight leaves the airport. They give you a good chance of dying quick, and a better chance of months of agony of torn flesh, smashed guts and splintered bones. Take it to your kindly dealer, and the service people look right through you until you grab one by the arm, and then he says: Come back a week from Tuesday. Make an appointment. Their billions of tons of excreted pollutants wither the leaves on the trees and sicken the livestock. We hate our cars, Detroit. Those of us who can possibly get along without them do so very happily. For those who can't, if there were an alternate choice, they'd grab it in a minute. We buy them reluctantly and try to make them last, and they are not friendly machines anymore. They are expensive, murderous junk, and they manage to look glassily contemptuous of the people who own them. A car is something that makes you whomp your youngest kid too hard and then feel ashamed of yourself. [John D. MacDonald, *Pale Gray for Guilt*.]

16th DAY

Telling Stories

Anecdotes often outlast their original point. They arouse curiosity, sympathy. They show us heroes and victims. They let us daydream. In fact, anecdotes seem like a relief from the hard work of listening to high thought. Unlike pages of logic, they do not seem to aim at proving anything—hence, their endings may surprise us with more meaning.

A well-told anecdote can serve to sharpen your main point; a shorter and livelier way of summing up what you have to say.

How does such a story fit into a larger piece of writing? It should reveal your character. It should *seem* like a distraction. It should give us a glimpse of real life, suggesting more than your main argument.

Very well. But what makes a story "well told"? No one knows. Here are some suggestions—strategies that we see many storytellers use. If your story has some emotional force, then you may be able to strengthen its impact by carrying out one or another of these rules:

- Relate events in chronological order.
- Focus on conflict: person against person, man against circumstances, idea against idea.
- Choose a character with an aim: and obstacles.
- Concentrate on one or two characters, not more.
- Do allow irrational—and irrelevant—elements.
- Use your words for talk and action—not scenery.
- Surprise, but reward, our expectations.

Even if all these rules are followed, remember, they cannot bring a dull story to life. Your own gut reaction is crucial to your choice of anecdotes: what you think is funny, astonishing, or tragic. See if you feel a particular story *has* to be told.

Realize that your reader looks on stories as clues to your emotional makeup: what you like and don't like, what moves you. You may feel an injustice; the reader sees that, and your anger. For instance, see what emotions Bruce Catton cherishes in this excerpt from his history of the Civil War:

> In the Shenandoah Valley, Union soldiers were learning that southern civilians could be exactly like the folks at home and that there could be a touch of friendship now and then between the invaders and the invaded. The 13th

Massachusetts was appealed to by a valley farmer for protection against for-
agers, and the colonel detailed four men to guard the place. The farmer insisted that they stay in the house and make themselves comfortable; he
would go about his duties and would call them if any prowlers appeared. His
wife would not let them bunk down in the yard when night came, but put
them in bedrooms with soft mattresses and clean white sheets, told them to
sleep until they were called in the morning, served breakfast at eight-thirty—
hominy and bacon, potatoes and fried chicken, hot biscuits and coffee, all
they could eat. When the regiment finally had to move on and the detail was
called away, the farmer went to the colonel to testify what fine young men
these soldiers were, and his wife sent a huge basket of biscuits and cakes for
them to take with them. All the rest of the war the 13th Massachusetts
nursed this memory. [*This Hallowed Land.*]

Because Catton chose to relate this incident, which suggests that even in the
middle of war some people could stay human, we get a feeling for the author too.

So when you're pondering stories, think what emotions they bring up in you—
and ask yourself if you want your audience attributing those feelings to you.

EMOTIONAL WORKOUT

Describe two incidents that have happened in your general neighborhood, one
that pleased you, one that irritated you. Let's imagine these will fit into a longer
essay about your neighborhood's character. After you've written them, jot down
what emotion seemed predominant.

_____

_____

_____

_____

_____

_____

_____

_____

_____

_____

Of course your story should prove something—your main point. But at the
same time, realize that your readers enjoy getting off the point, wandering
around in a good story about another time and place. For instance, when reporters kept asking him what would happen next in the quarrel between North and
South, Lincoln seemed to amble off the subject:

When I was a young lawyer, and Illinois was little settled, I, with other lawyers, used to ride the circuit. Once a long spell of pouring rain flooded the

whole country. Ahead of us was the Fox River, larger than all the rest, and we could not help saying to each other, "If these small streams give us so much trouble, how shall we get over Fox River?" Darkness fell before we had reached that stream, and we all stopped at a log tavern, had our horses put up, and resolved to pass the night. Here we were right glad to fall in with the Methodist Presiding Elder of the circuit, who rode it in all weather, knew all its ways, and could tell us all about Fox River. So we all gathered around him, and asked him if he knew about the crossing of the Fox River. "O yes," he replied, "I know all about Fox River. I have crossed it often, and understand it well. But I have one fixed rule with regard to Fox River: *I never cross it till I reach it!*

Lincoln could have answered, "I'll cross that bridge when I come to it," but then the reporters could have popped up again, saying, "But ... but ... but ..." This way Lincoln distracted them, lulled them into listening, focusing anxiety on crossing the Fox River. Only after these detours did he get to his italicized point—making the story seem apt, and, in the end, relevant.

The detour, though, not the ultimate destination, is what often appeals to readers. A story is a treat: it draws children from their play, and makes old men turn from the fireplace. We like to lose ourselves in the dark night and the rain—through fiction. So help our imagination, by developing those little side details, the extras that persuade us it really happened.

PROVERBIAL WISDOM

Think of a proverb, then imagine some story that might prove it. After you have the rough plot in mind, write it out at paragraph length, putting yourself into it, and including numerous concrete details—even if you're making them up.

Proverb: _____

Basic story: _____

_____

Your personal version: _____

_____

_____

_____

_____

_____

_____

_____

_____

When we write, our mind tends to stick to the point, and for that, many facts seem incidental, almost irrelevant. But for a reader, one of those stray details may make the whole scene come alive. An idle fact can give a flash picture of a person's way of life or culture. *That,* really, seems more important to the reader than the ultimate message.

So choose stories that suggest more than your point, by creating a sense of place, or giving new insights into the paradox of someone's personality, or showing glimpses of unusual activities. Here, for instance, is Ben Franklin explaining that Indians disagree with white folk about what makes an education valuable. Notice, though, that he sets up a whole scene, going beyond the simple theme to describe their manners, and that he quotes them with respect:

> Our laborious manner of life, compared with theirs, they esteem slavish and base; and the learning, on which we value ourselves, they regard as frivolous and useless. An instance of this occurred at the treaty of Lancaster, in Pennsylvania, anno 1744, between the government of Virginia and the Six Nations. After the principal business was settled, the commissioners from Virginia acquainted the Indians by a speech that there was at Williamsburg a college, with a fund for educating Indian youth; and that, if the chiefs of the Six Nations would send down half a dozen of their sons to that college, the government would take care that they should be well provided for, and instructed in all the learning of the white people. It is one of the Indian rules of politeness not to answer a public proposition the same day that it is made; they think it would be treating it as a light matter, and that they show it respect by taking time to consider it, as of a matter important. They therefore deferred their answer till the day following; when their speaker began by expressing their deep sense of the kindness of the Virginia government, in making them that offer; "for we know," says he, "that you highly esteem the kind of learning taught in those colleges, and that the maintenance of our young men, while with you, would be very expensive to you. We are convinced, therefore, that you mean to do us good by your proposal; and we thank you heartily. But you, who are wise, must know that different nations have different conceptions of things; and you will therefore not take it amiss, if our ideas of this kind of education happen not to be the same with yours. We have had some experience of it; several of our young people were formerly brought up at the colleges of the northern provinces; they were instructed in all your sciences; but, when they came back to us, they were bad runners, ignorant of every means of living in the woods, unable to bear either cold or hunger, knew neither how to build a cabin, take a deer, nor kill an enemy, spoke our language imperfectly, were therefore neither fit for hunters, warriors, nor counsellors; they were totally good for nothing. We are however not less obliged by your kind offer, though we decline accepting it; and, to show our grateful sense of it, if the gentlemen of Virginia will send us a dozen of their sons, we will take great care of their education, instruct them in all we know, and make *men* of them. [*Remarks on the Politeness of the Savages of North America.*]

What if your stories aren't original? Abe Lincoln, who was considered a great storyteller, claimed he borrowed most of his: "I remember a good story when I hear it, but I never invented anything original. I am only a retail dealer." But he did make a habit of memorizing jokes and tales when he heard them. And he felt free to cook up new circumstances for old plots.

Do the stories have to be true? It depends on what you claim. Comedians, for instance, hardly claim that everything they say is true, so we do not hold them to legal standards of veracity. But if you claim something happened to you just last week, we'll take that as a claim that you *are* telling the truth. And if you don't, we'll probably get the scent of the lie. If you simply make up some story to prove your general thesis, your audience will feel distaste, without knowing quite why. Yes, truth helps. But truth includes fiction: a fiction writer, like the joke teller, admits that he does not—cannot—tell the whole truth, and that what he presents is his own subjective vision. In that sense, he may be more honest than the writer who claims he deals just in facts.

A TASTE TEST FOR TRUTH

Tell some incident you remember from childhood—something you've remembered many times. Perhaps a moment in the first years of school. Then make up something that did not actually happen, but that might have, to prove the general point that "we learn from doing, not hearing." Then taste the difference between the two anecdotes.

A. _____

_____

_____

_____

_____

B. _____

_____

_____

_____

_____

An anecdote should help you prove your main point, but the point should not overwhelm the story, wiping out the irrelevant details that give it color and excitement. However, by the end of the story—or just after it—we should be able to understand why you thought of it in connection with your larger purpose. Allan Swenson tells us that we don't have to be Paul Bunyan to cut, split, and stack wood:

> Cutting with a chain saw is easier than with the hand saws of the old days. If you wish to be a purist in that regard, the pleasure and sweat can be yours, but chain saws are obviously faster, easier, and more reliable, and they cut through much more wood per day than you could by hand. The story is told of the neophyte who had never used one. He asked the clerk in the hardware store how many trees he might cut per day with the chain saw he intended to purchase. Twenty or thirty, the clerk replied, and the man gladly bought the saw. He was back the next day after spending a full day in the woods. Throwing the saw on the store counter, he complained that he had been able to cut only three trees in a full day. The clerk was amazed. He picked up the saw, turned on the switch and yanked the starter cord. The saw burst to life with a roar.
> "What's that noise?" the neophyte woodsman asked.

That story has made the rounds more than a few times, especially at woodsmen's gatherings. There really is a point to it. When you buy a chain saw, ask for a demonstration to learn how it works. Then test it yourself, if possible. Be certain to read the manual carefully and be sure you understand the directions. [*Wood Heat.*]

Anecdotes help us sum up our ideas: from one event, we can draw many conclusions—or the same one, over and over. Stories also bring up painful emotions, show us glimpses of unfamiliar lives, and let us dream awake. Still, we may hesitate before inserting a good story.

When should we bring in an anecdote?

- Whenever we find our text becoming too reasonable, too logical, too factual: in a word, too dull.
- Whenever we want to sum up a complex idea.
- Whenever we want an image to distill our argument.
- Whenever we want to amuse or distract the reader.
- Whenever we want to gossip about human beings.

And as we contemplate an anecdote, wondering whether to include it or not, we might ask it a series of questions:

- Does it prove my point?
- Does it begin by seeming to wander away from the point?
- Does it give us a glimpse of something more than just the point?
- Is it true? (And do I claim it is?)
- Does it bring up emotions I feel strongly?
- And, at the beginning or end, have I shown, clearly, how it does prove my point?

SOME OTHER ANECDOTES

THOSE despatches don't mean anything. The Governor is like a boy I saw once at a launching. When everything was ready they picked out a boy and sent him under the ship to knock away the trigger and let her go. At the critical moment everything depended on the boy. He had to do the job well by a direct, vigorous blow, and then lie flat and keep still while the ship slid over him. The boy did everything right, but he yelled as if he were being murdered from the time he got under the keel until he got out. I thought the hide was all scraped off his back; but he wasn't hurt at all. The master of the yard told me that this boy was always chosen for that job, that he did his work well, that he never had been hurt, but that he always squealed in that way. That's just the way with Governor Blank. Make up your minds that he is not hurt, and that he is doing his work right, and pay no attention to his squealing. He only wants to make you understand how hard his task is, and that he is on hand performing it. [Abe Lincoln, quoted in Carl Sandburg's, *Abraham Lincoln.*]

I KNOW another aged Indian, with his only daughter and wife alone in their lodge. He had a few beaver skins and four or five poor horses—all he had. The night was bad and held every stream in thick ice; the earth was white; the stars burned nearer us as if to pity us, but the more they burned the more stood the hair of the deer on end with cold, nor heeded they the frost bursting the willows. Two of the white man's people came to the lodge, lost and freezing pitifully. They fared well inside that lodge. The old wife and only daughter unbound and cut off their frozen shoes, gave them new ones, and crushed sage bark rind to keep their feet smooth and warm. They gave them warm soup, boiled deer meat and boiled beaver. They were saved; their safety returned to make them live. After a while they would not stop; they would go. They went away. Mind you: remember well! At midnight they returned, murdered the old father and his daughter and her mother asleep, took the beaver skins and horses, and left. Next day the first and only Indian they met, a fine young man, they killed, put his body under the ice and rode away on his horse.

Yet they say *we* are not good! [Chief Charlot, quoted in *The Weekly Missoulian*, Montana, April 26, 1876.]

17th DAY
Unifying Each Paragraph

A paragraph is a useful unit. With each new paragraph, you can take your argument one step forward, adding one idea, one insight, to our general understanding of your subject.

So, to help us move easily through your pages, assign each paragraph its own subject, and, no matter how many topics you mention in it, unify that paragraph into a single unit of thought.

A unified paragraph can be understood quickly; it acts like a basket, collecting all the ideas that relate to its main point, leaving out any that do not apply; and, at the end, it spills toward the next paragraph, suggesting what is to come.

You risk losing your reader whenever the sentences in a paragraph leap from one idea to another, without obvious connections, jump around in time and space, out of sequence, or wander far away from the paragraph's central point. To avoid confusing the reader, then, focus each paragraph on one central subject, make a distinct point, emphasize whatever makes the structure coherent, and show the links between one sentence and the next.

When you are planning a page, it seems easy to divide your subject up into its parts or stages, assigning a paragraph to each. But once you start writing, you may find yourself anticipating what you will say later, or remembering what you should have said a few pages back, or wondering whether the material you had planned to bring in two pages later might not really belong here.

That's the time for a scalpel. Ask yourself: what is the main subject in this paragraph? What *has* to go with that? And what else can be pared away?

You may find you have three paragraphs bound up together as one. If so, open up your text with paragraph marks like this: ¶ These pauses divide your writing into discrete, visible units, making each one easier to digest. Remember, long paragraphs *look* complicated; short ones, easy.

BREAKING UP THE TERRITORY

Here is a leisurely paragraph on the land of Great Britain—its weather, its material wealth, its game, and its dark skies. Divide the passage into four paragraphs by pencilling in ¶.

The territory has a singular perfection. The climate is warmer by many degrees than it is entitled to by latitude. Neither hot nor cold, there is no hour in the whole year when one cannot work. Here is no winter, but such days as we have in Massachusetts in November, a temperature which makes no exhausting demand on human strength, but allows the attainment of the largest stature. Charles the Second said, "It invited men abroad more days in the year and more hours in the day than another country." Then England has all the materials of a working country except wood. The constant rain—a rain with every tide, in some parts of the island—keeps its multitude of rivers full and brings agricultural production up to the highest point. It has plenty of water, of stone, of potter's clay, of coal, of salt and of iron. The land naturally abounds with game; immense heaths and downs are paved with quails, grouse, and woodcock, and the shores are animated by water-birds. The rivers and the surrounding sea spawn with fish; there are salmon for the rich and sprats and herrings for the poor. In the northern lochs, the herring are in innumerable shoals; at one season, the country people say, the lakes contain one part water and two parts fish. The only drawback on this industrial conveniency is the darkness of its sky. The night and day are too nearly of a color. It strains the eye to read and to write. Add the coal smoke. In the manufacturing towns, the fine soot or *blacks* darken the day, give white sheep the color of black sheep, discolor the human saliva, contaminate the air, poison many plants and corrode the monuments and buildings. [Emerson, "On England."]

Once you have isolated your subject—put in everything that belongs there and left out the unrelated items—you face the challenge of organizing the details within the paragraph. Often you can use a structure the reader finds familiar, even if he is not conscious that he recognizes it. For instance, you might arrange the contents of the paragraph as:

- A main idea, then proofs.
- One effect, and several causes.
- An extended contrast.
- Step by step through time or space.

Here, for example, Adam Smith sketches the rural economy, stating his point at the start, then laying on proofs:

When the market is very small, no person can have any encouragement to dedicate himself entirely to one employment, for want of the power to exchange all that surplus part of the produce of his own labor, which is over and above his own consumption, for such parts of the produce of other men's labor as he has occasion for. In the lone houses and very small villages which are scattered about in so deserted a country as the Highlands of Scotland, every farmer must be butcher, baker, and brewer for his own family. In such situations we can scarce expect to find even a smith, a carpenter, or a mason, within less than twenty miles of another of the same trade. The scattered families that live at eight or ten miles distance from the nearest of them must learn to perform themselves a great number of little pieces of work, for which, in more populous countries, they would call in the assistance of those workmen. Country workmen are almost everywhere obliged to apply themselves to all the different branches of industry that have so much affinity to one another as to be employed about the same sort of materials. A country carpenter deals in every sort of work that is made of wood: a country smith in every sort of work that is made of iron. The former is not only a carpenter, but a joiner, a cabinet-maker, and even a carver in wood, as well as a wheelwright, a plough-wright, a cart and waggon-maker. The employments of the latter are still more various. It is impossible there should be such a trade as even that of a nailer in the remote and inland parts of the Highlands of Scotland. Such a workman at the rate of a thousand nails a day, and three hundred working days in the year, will make three hundred thousand nails in the year. But in such a situation it would be impossible to dispose of one thousand, that is, of one day's work in the year. [Adam Smith, *The Wealth of Nations*.]

When Mark Twain started to explain how much a Mississippi river pilot had to know, he decided to compare the river with a very long street. He sketched out in general terms how much information was needed; then pinned down how precise, how small the details would be; then underlined the way those minute facts would change from month to month. So he structured his paragraph as an extended contrast, and within that, moved rapidly from general knowledge to detailed information. Notice that movement within the structure:

One cannot easily realize what a tremendous thing it is to know every trivial detail of twelve hundred miles of river and know it with absolute exactness. If you will take the longest street in New York, and travel up and down it, conning its features patiently until you know every house and window and door and lamp post and big and little sign by heart, and know them so accurately that you can instantly name the one you are abreast of when you are set down at random in that street in the middle of an inky black night, you will then have a tolerable notion of the amount and exactness of a pilot's knowledge who carries the Mississippi River in his head. And then, if you will go on until you know every street-crossing, the character, size, and position of the crossing-stones, and the varying depth of mud in each of those numberless places, you will have some idea of what the pilot must know in order to keep a Mississippi steamer out of trouble. Next, if you will take half of the signs in that long street, and *change their places* once a month, and still manage to know their new positions accurately on dark nights, and keep up with these repeated changes without making any mistakes, you will understand what is required of a pilot's peerless memory by the fickle Mississippi. [*Life on the Mississippi*.]

Twain leads off with his main idea, proves it, then proves it even more strongly, and finally astonishes us with one amazing last proof. That organization helps us move through a fair amount of raw data, without getting lost in the mud.

GIVING STRUCTURE TO PUDDING

Imagine you are about to write a paragraph about pudding. Any kind of pudding. Organize the paragraph as a main idea with proofs; then as an effect coming from several causes; then as a point-by-point comparison with something else.

A. Pudding: main idea: _____

One-sentence proofs: 1. _____

_____

2. _____

3. _____

B. Pudding: the effect: _____

   One-sentence causes: 1. _____

   _____

   2. _____

   3. _____

C. Pudding vs. _____ : Pudding is . . . _____

   but _____ is _____.

   One-sentence comparisons: 1. _____

   _____

   2. _____

   3. _____

In high school, we heard a lot about topic sentences. Terrible phrase, because the opening sentence should do more than simply announce a topic: it should state your main idea for that paragraph. You hardly need to start every paragraph with a topic sentence, but occasionally it helps. Then we can read through the rest of the paragraph, looking for evidence to back up your opinion. A good opening sentence can suggest the way you have arranged the rest of the paragraph; for instance, you may tell us that you are going to compare a river to a street, or to explain the causes of the Chinese Revolution, or to trace the growth of a tree. Right off, we know what kind of structure to expect in the rest of the paragraph—and as long as you deliver on that promise, we find it easy reading.

OPENING UP THE PUDDINGS

Write the opening sentences for each of the paragraphs you organized above.

A. _____

   _____.

B. _____

   _____.

C. _____

   _____.

Within a longish paragraph, you may want to resort to words that differentiate the important from the unimportant, the first from the last, or emphasize the actual progress of events. For instance, you may emphasize that you are organizing your information in spatial sequence by using words like *across, along, up, down,* and *around.* Robert Louis Stevenson started a trip into the deserted parts of a Pacific island this way:

> Well, this kind of talk put in the evening, which was the best of it; but of
> course it didn't change my notion, and the next day, with my gun and a good

knife, I set off upon a voyage of discovery. I made, as near as I could, for the place where I had seen Case come out; for if it was true he had some kind of establishment in the bush I reckoned I should find a path. The beginning of the desert was marked off by a wall, to call it so, for it was more of a long mound of stones. They say it reaches right across the island, but how they know it is another question, for I doubt if any one has made the journey in a hundred years, the natives sticking chiefly to the sea and their little colonies along the coast, and that part being mortal high and steep and full of cliffs. Up to the west side of the wall the ground has been cleared, and there are cocoa-palms and mummy-apples and guavas, and lots of sensitive plants. Just across, the bush begins outright; high bush at that, trees going up like the masts of ships, and ropes of liana hanging down like a ship's rigging, and nasty orchids growing in the forks like funguses. The ground where there was no underwood looked to be a heap of boulders. I saw many green pigeons which I might have shot, only I was there with a different idea. A number of butterflies flopped up and down along the ground like dead leaves; sometimes I would hear a bird calling, sometimes the wind overhead, and always the sea along the coast. [*The Beach of Falesa.*]

If you want to show that each of your examples carries about the same weight, you might use words like *similarly, likewise, furthermore*. But if one example stands out, then you might make that clear by using *mainly, primarily,* or *most importantly*. Or if you are organizing a series of causes, you may want to use words that suggest logical connections between them: *thus, so, then, therefore,* and *hence*.

Use signpost words only when the link between one sentence and the next might be unclear. Too many of these words can slow the reader down or baffle him. Used with restraint, though, these words help direct the reader forward by making the structure clear.

SPOTLIGHTING THE SIGNPOSTS

Circle the words that Robert Louis Stevenson uses to show us how one item adds to another in his backpack:

First there was that Bible, a book as big as your head, which I had let myself in for by my own tomfoolery. Then there was my gun, and knife, and lantern, and patent matches, all necessary. And then there was the real plant of the affair in hand, a mortal weight of gunpowder, a pair of dynamite fishing-bombs, and two or three pieces of slow match that I had pulled out of the tin cases and spliced together the best way I could; for the match was only trade stuff, and a man would be crazy that trusted it. Altogether, you see, I had the materials of a pretty good blow-up! Expense was nothing to me; I wanted that thing done right. [*The Beach of Falesa.*]

There are other ways of unifying your paragraphs, and we have mentioned some of them before: in a paragraph you can tell a whole story, explore a parallel or contrast, or repeat a brief conversation. Or you can turn to an image to tie together the details that might otherwise challenge description, as Thoreau does:

Cape Cod is the bared and bended arm of Massachusetts; the shoulder is at Buzzard's Bay; the elbow, or crazy-bone, at Cape Mallebarre; the wrist at Truro; and the sandy fist at Provincetown—behind which the state stands on her guard, with her back to the Green Mountains, and her feet planted on the floor of the ocean, like an athlete protecting her Bay—boxing with northeast storms, and, ever and anon, heaving up her Atlantic adversary from the lap of the earth—ready to thrust forward her other fist which keeps guard the while upon her breast at Cape Ann. [*Cape Cod.*]

IMAGINING YOUR STATE

What does the outline of your state look like on the map? Compare it to something we can see, and lead us around the edges, helping us to "see" it better. Choose an image that suggests your attitude toward your state.

_____

_____

_____

_____

_____

You *can* repeat yourself. Saying the same thing over and over gets boring, and makes the reader exit. But using the same word to say new things about the same subject does not have to be boring; it can, in fact, be a way of satirizing someone you don't like, as the novelist Charles Dickens does:

> Mr. and Mrs. Veneering were bran-new people in a bran-new house in a bran-new quarter of London. Everything about the Veneerings was spick and span new. All their furniture was new, all their friends were new, all their servants were new, their plate was new, their carriage was new, their harness was new, their horses were new, their pictures were new, they themselves were new, they were as newly married as was lawfully compatible with their having a bran-new baby, and if they had set up a great-grandfather, he would have come home in matting from the Pantechnicon, without a scratch upon him, French polished to the crown of his head. [*Our Mutual Friend.*]

By using the word *new* over and over, Dickens shows his attitude toward the Veneerings. The repetitions begin to sneer.

A coherent paragraph rarely draws attention to itself, whereas the straggling, meandering, or tangled paragraph irritates the reader so much that he notices the words, not the meaning underneath, for the chaotic mess of sentences bogs him down, makes him wonder what the point is and where the whole thing is headed.

But a unified paragraph helps the reader move forward quickly. He sees what the subject is, and what the point is, he knows where to look for proof, he grasps what the structure will be, he sees why one sentence leads into the next. As a result, he can begin to think about what you have to say, and how it fits in with what you have already discussed, rather than spending time and energy figuring out where you are going.

So, to maintain your momentum, be clear, and make sure your every paragraph is unified. How?

- Focus on one subject.
- Make your structure clear.
- Emphasize your main idea.
- Use linking words and signposts.
- Organize around an image or a story.
- Dare to repeat yourself.

POINTED PARAGRAPHS

ON the morning of July 2, I sat on San Juan Hill and watched Lawton's division come up. I was absolutely sheltered, but still where I could look into the faces of men who were trotting up under fire. There wasn't a high heroic face among them. They were all men intent on business. That was all. It may seem to you that I am trying to make everything a squalor. That would be wrong. I feel that things were often sublime. But they were differently sublime. They were not of our shallow and preposterous fictions. They stood out in a simple, majestic commonplace. It was the behavior of men on the street. It was the behavior of men. In one way, each man was just pegging along at the heels of the man before him, who was pegging along at the heels of still another man who—. It was that in the flat and obvious way. In another way it was pageantry, the pageantry of the accomplishment of naked duty. One cannot speak of it—the spectacle of the common man serenely doing his work, his appointed work. [Stephen Crane, "Wounds in the Rain"]

HIS motions plainly denoted his extreme exhaustion. In most land animals there are certain valves of flood-gates in many of their veins, whereby when wounded, the blood is in some degree at least instantly shut off in certain directions. Not so with the whale; one of whose peculiarities it is, to have an entire non-valvular structure of the blood-vessels, so that when pierced even by so small a point as a harpoon, a deadly drain is at once begun upon his whole arterial system; and when this is heightened by the extraordinary pressure of water at a great distance below the surface, his life may be said to pour from him in incessant streams. Yet so vast is the quantity of blood in him, and so distant and numerous its interior fountains, that he will keep thus bleeding and bleeding for a considerable period; even as in a drought a river will flow, whose source is the well-springs of far-off and indiscernible hills. Even now, when the boats pulled upon this whale, and perilously drew over his swaying flukes, and the lances were darted into him, they were followed by steady jets from the new made wound, which kept continually playing, while the natural spout-hole in his head was only at intervals, however rapid, sending its afrighted moisture into the air. From this last vent no blood yet came, because no vital part of him had thus far been struck. His life, as they significantly call it, was untouched. [Herman Melville, *Moby Dick.*]

18th DAY

Being Logical

Whenever we write, we reason. We may make our thought processes obvious, or we may try to hide them, but they shine through the words. And if they do not make sense, the reader will begin to feel uneasy. He may not at first spot the error or the injustice in what we say, but he will withdraw acceptance.

As you work out your first draft, you may want to reexamine your own reasoning, to make sure it passes the crude but strenuous tests of common sense. Are your basic assumptions valid? Do you recognize them all? If some are hidden, are those also true? And if so, does your evidence match those assumptions, too? And do your conclusions really flow from your premises and your evidence?

At first glance, your writing may seem quite logical but thin. You may feel sudden leaps in the sense, skimpy sections, tenuous connections. In some parts, you may appeal to sheer emotion, in other parts, to an authority in another field—suggesting you lack proof.

Time to put your argument to some simple tests. Are you, perhaps, assuming more than you can prove, right at the beginning?

Here, for instance, Virginia Woolf explains why there were so few outstanding women writers in the Renaissance:

> It is unthinkable that any woman in Shakespeare's day should have had Shakespeare's genius. For genius like Shakespeare's is not born among laboring, uneducated, servile people. It was not born in England among the Saxons and the Britons. It is not born today among the working classes. How, then, could it have been born among women whose work began . . . almost before they were out of the nursery, who were forced to it by their parents and held to it by all the power of law and custom? [*A Room of One's Own.*]

What is her basic argument? That geniuses are never born to the working class; that women have always been laborers; and, therefore, no woman could ever be born a genius. She assumes, then, that the working class never turns out geniuses. That seems dubious, on the face of it. In addition, she talks as if upper-class women had to stoop to labor at the court of Queen Elizabeth: not true. Since both premises seem weak, her overall conclusion wavers. It may be true, but upon examination, it looks like the snobbery of the well-off bourgeoise.

Or regard John Milton, explaining the purpose of education:

> The end, then, of learning is to repair the ruins of our first parents by regaining to know God aright, and out of that knowledge to love him, to imitate him, to be like him, as we may the nearest by possessing our souls of true virtue, which, being united to the heavenly grace of faith, makes up the highest perfection. ["Of Education."]

Pious as this is, a modern may doubt Milton's premise that the whole point of education is to set right original sin. And if that assumption is not already shared by the reader, then he may also hesitate before Milton's outline of the technique and aim of schooling.

Our premises tend to reflect our own era, class, and culture. Often, the stronger we hold to these beliefs, the odder they seem to people who come from outside our group.

So contemplate your own assumptions. First of all, try to write them out baldly and clearly, on a separate sheet of paper. Ask yourself: what other ones hide behind these? Pursue your premises, until you have gotten back to ideas that you are sure anyone—even someone from another nation or period—would agree to. Then challenge those.

Of course you are usually not writing for all time. So you need only examine the assumptions of your own culture, to see if they are really true. If you do this early enough in note-taking, you may discover a new perspective.

An American told his French wife she had to watch the baseball game.

"Eh, but why?"

"It's the World Series."

"Oh, is France playing?"

"No, just American teams."

"Well, why do they call it a World Series, then?"

"Because it's the championship—to see who's best, Philadelphia or Kansas City."

UNDERLINING ASSUMPTIONS

Look back through the conversation and underline an assumption the husband or the wife may be making. Spell it out below, and in a sentence explain why you doubt it, or agree.

_____

_____

_____

_____

_____

_____

Next, take apart your own assumptions, and look at the way you move from them to your conclusions. Do you, for instance, take a few examples, then jump to the conclusion that "they're all like that"? If so, you're assuming something else: that two apples show what the whole basket is like. Dubious again, but common. Why do we do this? To confirm a ready-made idea, to skip the hard work of proof—and, perhaps, to show off.

> A psychological reason for asserting "wild" generalizations is exhibitionism. The exhibitionist desires to attract attention to himself. No one pays much attention to such undramatic statements as "Some women are fickle," or that some are liars, or "Some politicians are no better than they ought to be." But when one says that "all women are liars," this immediately draws attention. Goethe once said that it is easy to appear brilliant if one respects nothing, not even the truth. [Lionel Ruby, *The Art of Making Sense.*]

For instance, arguing that wheat is more nutritious than oatmeal, Adam Smith makes a rapid comparison. He leaves out a hundred variables, attributing the whole difference between poor people in Scotland and England to the kind of bread they eat. An example of jumping to conclusions:

> In some parts of Lancashire it is pretended, I have been told, that bread of oatmeal is a heartier food for laboring people than wheaten bread, and I have frequently heard the same doctrine held in Scotland. I am, however, somewhat doubtful of the truth in it. The common people in Scotland, who are fed with oatmeal, are in general neither so strong, nor so handsome as the same rank of people in England, who are fed with wheat bread. [*The Wealth of Nations.*]

WHAT'S THE MISSING LINK HERE?

In the following passage, point out three of the unstated assumptions the author makes:

> Back in the Stone Age, hunters had no TV, no guns, no food processors. Lacking these, they must have felt their poverty, and worked frantically to kill enough deer, chop enough trees, gather enough nuts to be "well off." They must have felt frustration catching only one bull while a whole herd of buffalo thundered away. They must have envied squirrels their holes in trees; they must have dreamt of real houses, if they could imagine them. All in all, the Stone Age hunters must have felt intense anxiety.

1. _____

2. _____

3. _____

If you discredit these assumptions, what happens to the logic of the passage?

_____

_____

_____

Another way we sometimes move from our basic assumptions to our conclusion is through the either/or: we talk as if a person had only two options, so that if we can prove one impossible, we think we have proved he *must* choose the other. This line of thought, of course, ignores the human mind, always capable of coming up with some new way to do anything.

The number of such logical fallacies is infinite. You may, for instance, argue that just because something came after something else, it came because of it. (Not necessarily so.) Or you may avoid the whole question, and attack your opponent's character, implying that because he is immoral, his arguments *must* be false. You could spend years identifying and labeling different types of illogic—and in ancient Greece and Rome, that's just what the rhetoric teachers did.

They also developed a pattern for logical syllogisms. Our geometric theorems are the best example: a closed system, neatly defined premises, rules for proof, conclusions built on previously proved conclusions. Very neat, as long as your original premises are true: but of course, in outer space, they're not. So this geometry, accurate enought to build a skyscraper with, becomes incorrect when we fly from one planet to another. The proof may still be logically correct, but reality has outflanked it.

Pure logic, in fact, has little to do with reality. Words have to be defined so narrowly that they often fail to apply to anything in the world; the syllogism may be perfect, but ignore the facts. But common sense has its own more understanding logic—and that you can attain. To do so, though, you need to challenge your own assumptions—and the trail you take from them to your conclusions. You need to sift through your evidence repeatedly, asking yourself: is *this* what it adds up to? What else am I presuming about this material? What have I taken for granted? By analyzing the material in this way, you can bring to light the flaws in your own logic, and you may discover a smarter approach.

So when you suspect your writing's not too logical, sharpen your attitude; become dubious; challenge your proudest beliefs. Ask . . .

- What are my hidden premises?
- Are my assumptions valid?
- What facts have I left out of my argument?
- What evidence would be sufficient to prove this?
- Have I left out steps in my argument?
- Do I assume that what happens *after* happens *because of?*
- Do I assume that if it happens once, it happens always?
- Do I assume that it has to be either this or that, and not a third?
- What does common sense say?

REASONABLE EXAMPLES

COME, we shall have some fun now!" thought Alice. "I'm glad they've begun asking riddles. —I believe I can guess that," she added aloud.

"Do you mean that you think you can find out the answer to it?" said the March Hare.

"Exactly so," said Alice.

"Then you should say what you mean," the March Hare went on.

"I do," Alice hastily replied; "at least—at least I mean what I say—that's the same thing you know."

"Not the same thing a bit!" said the Hatter. "You might just as well say that 'I see what I eat' is the same thing as 'I eat what I see'!"

"You might just as well say," added the March Hare, "That 'I like what I get' is the same thing as 'I get what I like.'" [Lewis Carroll, *Alice's Adventures in Wonderland.*]

SHAKE off all the fears of servile prejudices, under which weak minds are servilely crouched. Fix reason firmly in her seat, and call on her tribunal for every fact, every opinion. Question with boldness even the existence of a God; because, if there be one, he must more approve of the homage of reason than that of blindfolded fear. [Thomas Jefferson, to his nephew.]

OUR dogmatists are lazy-bones. They refuse to undertake any painstaking study of concrete things, they regard general truths as emerging out of the void, they turn them into purely abstract unfathomable formulas, and thereby completely deny and reverse the normal sequence by which man comes to know truth. Nor do they understand the interconnection of the two processes of cognition—from the particular to the general and then from the general to the particular. [Mao Tse-tung, "On Contradiction."]

19th DAY

Attacking

Let's say you feel the urge to kill him, or at least to slam him into a wall. That old robber baron, Cornelius Vanderbilt wrote to one man, "You have undertaken to cheat me. I will not sue you because the law takes too long. I will ruin you."

Or if you want to tell someone that his letter is as worthless as toilet paper, write to him the way Voltaire did: "Dear Sir, I now sit in the smallest room in my house. I have your letter in front of me. Soon it will be behind me."

Attacking someone in a letter or report can ease your spleen, revive your liver, make you laugh, and help you get even. If someone has abused you, here's your chance to defend yourself. And if it's your job to evaluate employees, bosses, criminals, applicants, or clients, then you'll get paid to say why you don't like someone.

Since our culture spends so much effort telling us to be "nice," we often find it easier to praise than to condemn. It's not nice to attack, but it's fun—and cleansing. You can clear out a lot of stupidity by a loud assault. You can get justice done against criminals.

Still, when you find yourself about to write a report on someone, and you suspect—no, you know—that you don't approve, you face the unsettling feeling that *you* are at fault for saying so. And you suspect your audience may dislike you for being "mean." How to get past these objections?

Think of the fun of slaughter. P. G. Wodehouse once described a man as "A small shrivelled chap. Looks like a haddock with lung trouble." Or: Invited to address the stuffy women of the American Horticultural Society, Dorothy Parker pretended to misunderstand their organization's name: "You can lead a whore to culture," she smiled, "but you can't make her think." Anger can give you life, if you let it show.

Both writers reduced their victims—took away their dignity, and left them surprisingly shrunken, like pickled heads in Peru. Stephen Potter, the professor of one-upsmanship, tells us how to make our friends feel small: "It is an important general rule always to refer to your friend's country establishment as a 'cottage.'"

Call down disgust on your victim's head, too. William Golding sneered that one man was "as fitted to survive in this modern world as a tapeworm in an intestine."

Add shock to your weapons. A hundred years ago, you could startle anyone by breaking religious taboos—taking the Lord's name in vain, or mentioning human excrement in public. But such curses have become so commonplace that you need to surprise us by violating politeness. Conventional people ooh and ah over babies and pets—therefore we recall W. C. Fields' "impolite" statement: "Anybody who hates children and dogs can't be all bad." Most people think of their country as a parent: hence, to jolt his countrymen, James Joyce said, "Ireland is the old sow that eats her farrow."

Such jibes start out in a way that encourages us to complete the sentence in an insincere but "nice" way (anyone who hates kids . . . must be bad; Ireland is . . . our mother)—then offers us the opposite conclusion. The author tricks us, makes us stumble and listen.

Plausibility and accuracy drive in the stake. You can surprise us with a reversal of the expected: but we will agree with you if we feel, also, some recognition that what you say is true or, somehow, reflects what we really feel, too. Disappointed tourist, at a French château: "Nothing but thick walls and running commentary." Or the glamorous Zsa Zsa Gabor: "I never hated any man enough to give his diamonds back."

DARTS

You've seen dart boards made with pictures of people we love to hate. Think of some current villain, then badmouth that person four ways: make him seem small, disgusting; be impolite and accurate.

Small: _____

_____

Disgusting: _____

_____

Impolite: _____

_____

Accurate: _____

_____

If you can goad your opponent into openly abusing you, you will have set the stage for close work with your sword. A judge once meant to chastise a lawyer named Smith: "I have read your case, Mr. Smith, and I am no wiser now than I was when I started."

Mr. Smith's reply: "Possibly not, my Lord, but far better informed."

The judge got huffy. "You are offensive, sir."

"We both are," remarked Mr. Smith. "The difference is that I'm trying to be and you can't help it."

Such ripostes use the opponent's own weapon to wound him. You come off seeming an innocent defending yourself: he looks mean—and stupid. Two points for you.

If you feel the person you are about to attack has really forfeited any right to mercy, then you can still appear to listen, while shouting. Draw up a list of his main arguments; then go through each one, stating it, then knocking it down. The effect: you have heard each defense, and you have eliminated them. In such circumstances, you can dramatize the confrontation by admitting, not hiding, your intentions, by acting like a prosecutor wiping out each alibi.

What carries you through this kind of attack is the outrage underneath, the sheer emotion. Demagogues, stirring up half-drunk crowds, rely on passion, and even in apparently quiet offices, groups love to feel the intensity of your raw feeling. If you can let that show without sacrificing the give-and-take, the semblance of reasoning, you can condemn your enemy without appearing to do anything more than judge.

GETTING PERSONAL

Think of someone you dislike. First, put down three ideas he might maintain, on the left. Then, on the right, put your outraged responses. Finally, number them so that we can read them from least to most emotional.

IDEAS   RESPONSES

_____

_____

_____

Simple raving may satisfy you as you write it, but the results usually just turn your audience against you. What, for instance, do you think of the person who wrote this?

> God damn your god-damned old hell-fired god-damned soul to hell. God damn you and god damn your god damned family's god damned hellfired god damned soul to hell and good damnation god damn them and god damn your god damn friends to hell. [Letter to Abe Lincoln.]

You feel as if you could wipe the spit off the man's jowls. Similarly, the newspaper editors who joked about Lincoln as a third-rate country lawyer, a long-armed baboon who didn't know good grammar and told coarse stories, showed that they themselves valued sophistication more than good sense. One editor read the Gettysburg address, and could not stop himself from writing: "The cheek of every American must tingle with shame as he reads the silly, flat, and dishwatery utterances of the man who has to be pointed out to intelligent foreigners as the President of the United States." That doesn't say much about the speech, but it does show that the writer was a snob.

To avoid these extremes (spluttering and name-calling), take the time to pile up solid evidence. And along with facts (relevant or not), you may suggest motives. In this way, you help the reader imagine she understands your opponent's personality.

MOTIVATING AN ENEMY

Pick someone else who has offended you, irritated you, bothered you. Start describing that person's motives, then follow those impulses through the day, showing how they surface in speech and act. Leave your formal accusation to the end.

Avoid getting tangled up in a detailed answer to every charge an opponent has made against you. It takes a long time, and no one but you cares that much about what someone else said against you. Go for the sharp retort rather than the five-page rebuttal. Then you'll be heard. Once, when a music critic ridiculed Margaret Truman's piano playing, her father, the president, dismissed his rambling review by telling the critic: "You sound like an eight-ulcer man on a four-ulcer job." After that, who wants to bother reading the critique?

If you must let off hot air, scribble those long replies—but keep them in your desk. If you feel someone's driving you crazy, call them names—but, unless they make other people laugh, file the paper in your wastebasket.

Attacks develop force from wit and evidence: passion arouses us most when it passes through the brain before it comes out the mouth. Yes, yell and scream. Kill the bastard in your mind. But to win support for your motion to indict, be, or seem, reasonable.

How then, can you best attack?
- Make your victim look small.
- Arouse disgust.
- Risk being impolite.
- Turn your opponent's weapons against him.
- Make a show of "listening" to his views.
- Use evidence as ammunition.

- Suggest motives for his faults.
- Don't rant.

SHARP ATTACKS

It is better to die on our feet than live on our knees. [Emiliano Zapata.]

WHAT next? My God, why don't you break into our houses at night? Why don't you steal the watch out of my pocket, steal the horses out of the harness, hold us up with a shotgun; yes, 'stand and deliver; your money or your life.' Here we bring our ploughs from the East over your lines, but you're not content with your long-haul rate between Eastern points and Bonneville. You want to get us under your ruinous short-haul rate between Bonneville and San Francisco, *and return*. Think of it! Here's a load of stuff for Bonneville that can't stop at Bonneville, where it is consigned, but has got to go up to San Francisco first *by way of* Bonneville, at forty cents per ton and then be reshipped from San Francisco back to Bonneville again at *fifty-one* cents per ton, the short-haul rate. And we have to pay it all or go without. Here are the ploughs right here, in sight of the land they have got to be used on, the season just ready for them, and we can't touch them. Oh," he exclaimed in deep disgust, "isn't it a pretty mess! Isn't it a farce! the whole dirty business!" [Frank Norris, *The Octopus.*]

I DON'T make jokes—I just watch the government and report the facts. [Will Rogers.]

20th DAY

Defining

Money is like muck—not good unless it is spread.—Francis Bacon.

Money is like an arm or leg—use it or lose it.—Henry Ford.

Money is like a sixth sense—and you can't make use of the other five without it.—Somerset Maugham.

Money is the most important thing in the world. It represents health, strength, honor, generosity, and beauty as conspicuously as the want of it represents illness, weakness, disgrace, meanness and ugliness.—George Bernard Shaw.

As a cousin of mine once said about money, money is always there but the pockets change; it is not in the same pockets after a change, and that is all there is to say about money.—Gertrude Stein.

We know what money is, but the minute we begin to define it, we fight. Gold may be money, but money is not simply metal. It is not just the value written on a dollar bill. It can open palaces, kill whole cities, feed, clothe, house, and amuse us—and yet money itself does nothing.

So if you're about to write an analysis of the way cash flows across national borders, you will have to spell out precisely what you mean by the word *money*. Do you, for instance, include the daily change in value of real estate owned by people in one country, when it is not actually being sold?

Even if you are not writing about a subject as abused and admired as money, you may find you have to define your terms quite exactly. Perhaps you are using the words the reader does not know: phrases you have made up, jargon you have taken from some specialized field, foreign slang. Or perhaps you are using a word we all know, but only in one of its many meanings. If you do not define *which* of these meanings you are referring to, your reader may apply the other ones and become confused.

A good definition can be applied consistently throughout your piece of writing. But what if you change your mind as you go? Fine, then change your definition. In fact, expect that this will happen. Start with your best "working definition" of the terms you know will puzzle or irritate the reader. But as you write, consider whether that definition seems broad enough, narrow enough, accurate enough. Does it include everything you mean by that word? Does it clearly rule out other meanings? Does it identify the subject so well that it could apply *only* to that particular subject?

Defining is an extended process: you make up a definition, you test it out, you expand it, you limit it, perpetually refining it. Once you have a definition that will fit into every context you use in your paper, you can go back and insert the definition at the beginning.

Avoid dictionary quotes. Make up your own definition, so that it fits your meaning snugly. How? First figure out what general class your subject belongs in. Then figure out how it differs from all the other members of that class.

DEFINING OUR ROLES

Fill out this chart, to complete the definitions.

WORD	GENUS	DIFFERENCE
A roll is	a bread product that	_____.
A roll is	a physical move that	_____.
A role is	_____	we play, or adopt to disguise, or hide our own personality.
A pediatrician is	a doctor who	_____.
A podiatrist is	_____	fixes feet.
A gentleman is	a male who	_____

To make sure that the "difference" really distinguishes our subject from the others of its class, we may have to expand our definition beyond the length of a single sentence. How?
- By analyzing the subject's parts, or stages, or types.
- By excluding whatever it is not.
- By showing how it is used.
- By comparing and contrasting it with similar things.

When Melville tried to explain why a whale's tail is more than just a tail, he dissected its parts, finally comparing it to a wall:

> Reckoning the largest sized Sperm Whale's tail to begin at that point of the trunk where it tapers to about the girth of a man, it comprises upon its upper surface alone an area of at least fifty square feet. The compact round body of its root expands into two broad, firm, flat palms or flukes, gradually shoaling away to less than an inch in thickness. At the crotch of junction, these flukes slightly overlap, then sideways recede from each other like wings, leaving a wide vacancy between. In no living thing are the lines of beauty more exquisitely defined than in the crescentic borders of these flukes. At its utmost expansion in the full grown whale, the tail will considerably exceed twenty feet across.
>
> The entire member seems a dense webbed bed of welded sinews; but cut into it, and you find that three distinct strata compose it: upper, middle, lower. The fibres in the upper and lower layers, are long and horizontal; those of the middle one, very short, and running crosswise between the outside layers.

This triune structure, as much as anything else, imparts power to the tail. To the student of old Roman walls, the middle layer will furnish a curious parallel to the thin course of tiles always alternating with the stone in those wonderful relics of the antique, and which undoubtedly contribute so much to the great strength of the masonry. [*Moby Dick.*]

DEFINING

Define by listing the unique parts and materials:

———————— is a form of clothing . . . ————————————————

——

——

———————— is a vehicle . . . ————————————————

——

——

———————— is an animal . . . ————————————————

——

——

Now look back and see if you have given the details that distinguish your subject from all others in that class.

When British author Hilaire Belloc began to explain *Economics for Young People,* he wrote, "The economic definition of Wealth is subtle and difficult to appreciate. . . . First we must be clear as to what Wealth is *not*." Here, then, is a second route toward a definition. By ruling out anything that might be confused with our subject, we hope to leave our own subject clearly outlined. Saying what it is not can help define what our subject *is.*

WHAT IT'S NOT

Start out saying what your word does not mean; then, *at the end,* sum up what it does mean. Pick any three: self-defense, aggressiveness, ambition, hunger, anger, or money.

1. ——

——

——

2. ——

——

——

3. ——

As you put together a dossier on the unique parts, or stages, or types of your subject, excluding whatever does not belong, you may find yourself leaning toward a third method of definition: describing how your subject works—how it is used, how it grows, how it develops. Here, for instance, Ralph Waldo Emerson tells us how a beginner may grow—step by step—into a full "professor" of walking:

> No man is suddenly a good walker. Many men begin with good resolution, but they do not hold out, and I have sometimes thought it would be well to publish an Art of Walking, with Easy Lessons for Beginners. These we call apprentices. Those who persist from year to year, and obtain at last an intimacy with the country, and know all the good points within ten miles, with the seasons for visiting each, know the lakes, the hills, where grapes, berries, and nuts, where the rare plants are; where the best botanic ground; and where the noblest landscapes are seen, and are learning all the time—these we call professors. [*Country Life*]

Naturally, at some point, you may find you want to expand on your subject. And in that case, you may want to bring all three of these methods to bear—analyzing the subject's components, distinguishing it from similar subjects, describing it being used. And you may want to use fanciful imagery to give us an emotional impression: not what something is, but what it is *like*. Here, for instance, is an extended definition of *prayer*, using all four methods:

> Prayer is the peace of our spirit, the stillness of our thoughts, the evenness of recollection, the seat of meditation, the rest of our cares, and the calm of our tempest; prayer is the issue of a quiet mind, of untroubled thoughts, it is the daughter of charity and the sister of meekness; and he that prays to God with an angry, that is, with a troubled and discomposed spirit, is like him that retires into a battle to meditate, and sets up his closet in the outquarters of an army, and chooses a frontier-garrison to be wise in. Anger is a perfect alienation of the mind from prayer, and therefore is contrary to that attention which presents our prayers in a right line to God. For so have I seen a lark rising from his bed of grass; and soaring upwards, singing as he rises, and hopes to get to heaven, and climb above the clouds; but the poor bird was beaten back with loud sighings of an eastern wind, and his motion made irregular and unconstant, descending more at every breath of the tempest than it could recover by the libration and frequent weighing of his wings; till the little creature was forced to sit down and pant, and stay till the storm was over; and then it made a prosperous flight, and did rise as he passed sometimes through the air about his ministries here below. [Jeremy Taylor, *The Return of Prayers*.]

DEFINING A MOOD

Using all four methods of definition, try to pin down exactly what it feels like to you to be calm, reflective, or meditative. What goes on, inside and outside you?

What are the mood's components? How is it different from other similar feelings? And, in an image, what is it like?

_____

_____

_____

_____

_____

_____

_____

   The longer your definition, the more dangers you run, for a long definition runs the risk of being too broad, like a net that has holes in it—the fish escape. A short definition can be tested throughout your essay: in each case you can ask, could I substitute this phrase for the word, and still make sense? (Who can substitute a paragraph for a word?)

   Beware, too, of using the word you are defining in the definition. The dictionary makers do this, and drive us crazy. _Sexual_ means "of or pertaining to sex." Big help that is, when we want pictures.

   Your attitude toward your own definition should be tough. Bully it. Make sure it works: not just once, but every time you use the word. Your definition can be the strongest link in your argument, or the weakest. If you unconsciously use the word to mean one thing here, another there, a sharp reader will catch your inconsistency. Here, for instance, I've taken apart a Department of Labor definition of _occupation_ (as three months work that pays more than a third of one's income) in the way you might analyze your own first draft of a definition:

> An occupation? That's a job, we say. Well, yes, but does it mean a job we do full-time? Can part-time work as a soda jerk count as "an occupation"? Is serving on a corporation board once a month "an occupation"? Can a man do a job of work, and find that it does not count as an "occupation" if the government's DICTIONARY OF OCCUPATIONAL TITLES does not include what he did? And what about an apprentice? Does someone learning a trade truly have an "occupation"? Or do they just have a job? And does robbery constitute an occupation? How often do you have to practice embezzlement before that becomes your true occupation? Little wonder the committee settled on the wide-open definition: an occupation, to them, is any work that pays more than a third of your income for more than three months.

ATTACKING THE DICTIONARY

Look up a word in the dictionary, and take apart the definition. If possible, come up with a better one, more inclusive, more precise:

_____

_____

_____

A strong definition can act like the keystone in the arch of any argument. It can sum up most of what you have to say about the subject. It saves the reader minutes of effort, condensing much thought into a short sentence.

Whenever you feel a certain subject needs to be defined, then, you may want to answer these questions:

- What class of things does it belong to—and how is it different from all other members?
- How does it work? How is it used?
- What is it *not?*
- What is it like?
- What's wrong with other definitions?
- Am I using my own definition consistently?

MORE DEFINITIONS

As used in common discourse *wages* means a compensation paid to a hired person for his services; and we speak of one man "working for wages" in contra-distinction to another who is "working for himself." The use of the term is still further narrowed by the habit of applying it solely to compensation paid for manual labor. We do not speak of the wages of professional men, managers, or clerks, but their fees, commissions, or salaries. Thus the common meaning of the word *wages* is the compensation paid to a hired person for manual labor. But in political economy the word *wages* has a much wider meaning, and includes all returns for exertion. For, as political economists explain, the three agents or factors in production are land, labor, and capital, and that part of the produce which goes to the second of these factors is by them styled *wages.*

Thus the term *labor* includes all human exertion. . . . The gold washed out by the self-employing gold-digger is as much his wages as the money paid to the hired coal-miner by the purchaser of his labor, and, as Adam Smith shows, the high profits of retail store keepers are in large part wages, being the recompense of their labor and not of their capital. In short, whatever is received as the result or reward of exertion is *wages.* [Henry George, *Social Problems.*]

What is this nationality we are trying to preserve, this thing that we are fighting English influence to preserve? It is not merely our pride. It is certainly not any national vanity that stirs us on to activity. If you examine to the root a contest between two peoples, two nations, you will always find that it is really a war between two civilizations, two ideals of life. First of all, we Irish do not desire, like the English, to build up a nation where there shall be a very rich class and a very poor class. Ireland will always be in the main an agricultural country. Industries we may have, but we will not have, as England has, a very rich class, nor whole districts blackened with smoke like what they call in England their "Black Country." I think that the best ideal for our people, an ideal very generally accepted among us, is that Ireland is going to become a country where, if there are few rich, there shall be nobody very poor. Wherever men have tried to imagine a perfect life, they have imagined a place where men plow and sow and reap, not a place where there are great wheels turning and great chimneys vomiting smoke. Ireland will always be a country where men plow and sow and reap. [William Butler Yeats, speech.]

ACQUAINTANCE, n. A person whom we know well enough to borrow from, but not well enough to lend to. A degree of friendship called slight when its object is poor or obscure, and intimate when he is rich or famous.

BAROMETER, n. An ingenious instrument which indicates what kind of weather we are having.

CONNOISSEUR, n. A specialist who knows everything about something and nothing about anything else. An old wine-bibber having been smashed in a railway collision, some wine was poured upon his lips to revive him. "Pauillac, 1873," he murmured, and died.

MIRACLE, n. An act or event out of the order of nature and unaccountable, as beating a normal hand of four kings and an ace with four aces and a king. [Ambrose Bierce, *The Devil's Dictionary.*]

WHAT a piece of work is a man! How noble in reason! how infinite in faculty! in form, in moving, how express and admirable! in action how like an angel! in apprehension how like a god! the beauty of the world! the paragon of animals! And yet to me, what is this quintessence of dust? [William Shakespeare, *Hamlet,* act II, sc. ii.]

21st DAY

Nouns and Verbs,
not Adjectives and Adverbs

Adjectives powder and puff. Adverbs grease verbs, make them twist, turn, go faster, slower, up and down. But without a noun, no one's there, nothing can happen. And without a verb, the subject can't act, can't change, can't even *be*.

Nouns and verbs are the muscle and the motion of a sentence. You cannot have *red* without something underneath to *be* red—hence, nouns come first, and adjectives just qualify, color, and shade their nouns. Beautiful, yes, and subtle, but not essential. Often you can dispense with decoration altogether.

If you fill your paragraphs with fact and action, you give your readers the feeling that we can see and touch and taste what you describe. An occasional adjective may brighten a corner of the scene, or throw a general light across the whole. But the main work of creation, as we see in *Genesis,* takes place through spirit, matter, and motion—we only hear an adjective when God rests, and sees that it is good.

In writing done on the spot, in the heat of tears, we reach for nouns and verbs. You could say that people felt "nervous" when the South started the Civil War, but you would miss the quality of the experience. Here, for instance, Mary Chesnut tells of the night her neighbors fired the first shot on Fort Sumter:

> I do not pretend to go to sleep. Who can? If Anderson does not accept terms at four, the orders are he shall be fired upon. I count four, St. Michael's bells chime out, and I begin to hope. At half past four the heavy booming of a cannon. I sprang out of bed, and on my knees prostrate I prayed as I never prayed before.
>
> There was a sound of stir all over the house, pattering of feet in the corridors. All seemed hurrying one way. I put on my double gown and a shawl and went too. It was to the housetop. The shells were bursting. In the dark I heard a man say, "Waste of ammunition." I knew my husband was rowing a boat somewhere in that dark bay. If Anderson was obstinate, Colonel Chesnut was to order the fort on one side to open fire. Certainly fire had begun. The regular roar of the cannon, there it was. And who could tell what each volley accomplished of death and destruction?
>
> The women were wild there on the housetop. Prayers came from the women and imprecations from the men. And then a shell would light up the scene.

141

Tonight they say the forces are to attempt to land. We watched up there, and everybody wondered that Fort Sumter did not fire a shot.

We hear nothing, can listen to nothing: boom, boom, goes the cannon all the time. [*A Diary from Dixie.*]

Too many adjectives would have smothered that. Think of adjectives as paint: too much smears the picture, makes the figures hard to spot, brings attention to the medium, away from the subject. Look at all the adjectives in this description:

The day was fine. Since the first rain of the season, there had been no other. Now the sky was without a cloud, pale, blue, delicate, luminous, scintillating with morning. The great brown earth turned a huge flank to it, exhaling the moisture of the early dew. The atmosphere, washed clean of dust and mist, was translucent as crystal. Far off to the east, the hills on the other side of Broderson Creek stood out against the pallid saffron of the horizon as flat and as sharply outlined as if pasted on the sky. The campanile of the ancient Mission of San Juan seemed as fine as frost work. [Frank Norris, *Octopus.*]

We can feel Frank Norris struggle with that passage, adding one adjective, then another, then a dozen more, hoping they would give us some over-all effect. Norris could have cut some out, turned others into nouns or new sentences. What made the morning "scintillating"? How could he tell that the atmosphere was really "translucent as crystal"? Norris has not worked, he has not observed: he has generalized. And adjectives signal that laziness.

CLEANING OUT THE ADJECTIVES

Imagine you are the author of *The Octopus*, and you are about to rewrite the passage above; try to avoid instant generalizations and cut out adjectives by turning them into nouns or new sentences. If you want, add a person to the landscape.

_____

_____

_____

_____

The lazy way to define the Yiddish word *schlimazel* is to say it's someone who's *unlucky*. But just what kind of bad luck does he attract? What exactly does it mean? Leo Rosten explains by combining four folk sayings: "When a schlimazel winds a clock, it stops; when he kills a chicken, it walks; when he sells umbrellas, the sun comes out; when he manufactures shrouds, people stop dying."

In giving up adjectives, then, you do not have to give up complexity or tragedy. You may give up speed and ease in writing, but you help the reader understand you. More work for you—less for the reader.

ELIMINATING THE ADJECTIVES

Be dramatic. Cross out the adjectives in these sentences; then rewrite, saying the same thing with nouns and verbs, not adjectives. For "She became aggressive," you might write what you actually saw her do—"She hit Jimmy on the neck, screamed, 'You bastard!' and threw the bowl of grape jello on his feet."

She became even more aggressive: ————————————————————

————————————————————————————————

Even at twilight, the house stayed dark: ————————————————

————————————————————————————————

————————————————————————————————

She was friendly: ————————————————————————

————————————————————————————————

He talked vehemently about a number of slight, little, or unimportant things:

————————————————————————————————

————————————————————————————————

————————————————————————————————

Hiding within an adjective (describing the exact *kind* of object) or an adverb (describing the *way* something is done) you may find another sentence made up simply of nouns and verbs—or a series of sentences. In fact, whenever you press together too many adjectives, you may be condensing four sentences into one. Result: we can't follow your thought, step by step. You've run four thoughts into one. So if you notice your adjectives building up, ask yourself if you might not take more space and less fluff. How? Breathe more—and use more sentences.

For instance, a scholar might say that riding in a nineteenth-century stage-coach was "hard, athletic, sociable, close, and dark." That's true. But how much sinks in? From that list of qualities, what can we see, or feel? Here's how Mark Twain expanded on those conclusions:

> As the sun went down and the evening chill came on, we made preparation for bed. We stirred up the hard leather letter-sacks, and the knotty canvas bags of printed matter (knotty and uneven because of projecting ends and corners of magazines, boxes, and books). We stirred them up and redisposed them in such a way as to make our bed as level as possible. And we *did* improve it, too, though after all our work it had an upheaved and billowy look about it, like a little piece of a stormy sea. Next we hunted up our boots from odd nooks among the mailbags where they had settled, and put them on. Then we got down our coats, vests, pantaloons and heavy woolen shirts from the arm loops where they had been swinging all day, and clothed ourselves in them—for, there being no ladies either at the stations or in the coach, and the weather being hot, we had looked to our comfort by stripping to our un-

derclothing, at nine o'clock in the morning. All things being now ready, we stowed the uneasy Dictionary where it would lie as quiet as possible, and placed the water-canteens and pistols where we could find them in the dark. Then we smoked a final pipe, and swapped a final yarn; after which we put the pipes, tobacco, and bag of coin in snug holes and caves among the mail-bags, and then fastened down the coach curtains all around, and made the place as "dark as the inside of a cow," as the conductor phrased it in his picturesque way. It was certainly as dark as any place could be—nothing was even dimly visible in it. And finally, we rolled ourselves up like silk worms, each person in his own blanket, and sank peacefully to sleep. [*Roughing It.*]

Sir Thomas More was often merry. But again we cannot really appreciate what that meant until we know when, where, and what he thought about it—information that nouns and verbs give us.

> *Merry.* The word stayed ever on More's tongue and in his heart. To Dame Alice, he said, "I pray you with my children be merry in God." From the Tower during the last fifteen months of his life, he wrote to Margaret, "I beseech Him make you all merry in the hope of Heaven." The day before his execution he sent her the hair shirt and a letter written with a piece of coal: "To-morrow I long to go to God; it were a day very meet and convenient for me."
>
> On the morrow as he climbed the scaffold, which was weak and ready to fall, More said, "I pray you, Master Lieutenant, see me safe up, and for my coming down, let me shift for myself." By light words he took his leave. Without solemnity, with courtesy and compassion for others, with a cheerful serene face and three jests on the scaffold he went to die, speaking to the executioner, "Pluck up thy spirits, man, and be not afraid to do thine office. My neck is very short." He removed his beard from the block, "for it at least has not offended the king."
>
> The test of a man in the *Utopia* is the way he dies. Those who die "merrily and full of good hope, for them no man mourneth." They are praised for their merry death and monuments are erected to them. More showed how it was done. He died as he had lived. [Helen Bevington, *Beautiful Lofty People.*]

What did he do? What did he say? Those are the concerns that pull nouns and verbs out of your mind. Ernest Hemingway always claimed he smelled rot in any adjective; he tested most adjectives, and flunked them. He accused them of cheating, covering up, lying. He thought they let a writer coast.

If you focus on people and actions, your writing will gain strength. This is not a trick of style: it is an attitude toward truth, toward what matters. You could ape Hemingway's style but miss his power even if you clear out the descriptive words. What I am urging you to develop goes beyond words: it goes to the heart of the matter—what is felt beneath the words.

Once your heart is pure, then, the method is simple:

- Cut adjectives and adverbs.
- Use nouns and verbs.
- Replace adjectives and adverbs with new sentences.
- Focus on people, facts, and actions.

CLEAN WRITING

WITH malice toward none; with charity for all; with firmness in the right, as God gives us to see the right, let us strive on to finish the work we are in; to bind up the nation's wounds; to care for him who shall have borne the battle, and for his widow, and his orphan—to do all which may achieve and cherish a just and lasting peace among ourselves, and with all nations. [Abraham Lincoln, Second Inaugural Address.]

IN the beginning God created the heaven and the earth.

And the earth was without form, and void; and darkness was upon the face of the deep. And the Spirit of God moved upon the face of the waters.

And God said, Let there be light; and there was light.

And God saw the light, that it was good: and God divided the light from the darkness.

And God called the light Day, and the darkness he called Night. And the evening and the morning were the first day. [*Genesis,* King James version.]

22nd DAY

Active, Not Passive

But what kind of verbs? Active or passive? Loud or soft? Unruly or combed?

Our well-groomed middle-management executives tend to use passive verbs, because in the passive, no one is responsible (things are done; no one does them); tradition makes the rules (that is the way things *are* done), and the subject merely receives the shocks of the world around and above (being passive, he is ordered around, is rained on, is yelled at). In this interoffice memo, for instance, the writer eliminates names and acts—hence, although someone somehow has lost over $200,000 in the last two months, the writer talks as if "things just happened."

> The department is experiencing some cash-flow problems. Receipts are down 15 percent from last month; 5 percent of assets have already been drawn down; and $515,612.00 in bills are 60 days past due. There are no more than $312,111.00 on deposit, so the department is faced with priority-type decisions as to how such moneys are to be allocated.

In the passive world, a person merely is, or he absorbs the impulses of others. He does not *do*. He hardly exists. He has no will, and therefore very little responsibility. Hence, the passive verb seems most appropriate when the subject is a victim:

> After the revolution failed, 233 prisoners were tortured in the town plaza. First their legs were cut off at the thigh; then their arms were lopped off. Then ropes were tied around their necks and what was left of their torsos got dragged around the cobblestones until the faces were bloody mash. Only then were the soldiers permitted to shoot whichever body still twitched.

We tend to shift into the passive whenever we want to suggest that the subject has lost control—*is being* moved, rather than moves himself. *Is* also suggests a simple identity (the ax *is* sharp), or a state (the faces *were* bloody).

But active verbs suggest we can move, grow, fall; subjects of active verbs make change happen. Such verbs act like the drug in *Dr. Jekyll and Mr. Hyde*. In this passage from that story, the verbs rush in to suggest the speed of the transformation—then die out in past participles, as the witness stands frozen in terror:

> He put the glass to his lips, and drank at one gulp. A cry followed; he reeled, staggered, clutched at the table and held on, staring with injected eyes, gasping with open mouth; and as I looked, there came, I thought, a change—he seemed to swell—his face became suddenly black, and the features seemed to melt and alter—and the next moment I had sprung to my feet and leaped back against the wall, my arm raised to shield me from that prodigy, my mind submerged in terror. [Robert Louis Stevenson.]

Active verbs often suggest a decisive will at work. When Mao Tse-tung wrote to justify his guerrilla forces retreating he insisted that for a people's army, retreat is *not* passive; it becomes a turning path to victory. With liberal use of active verbs, he makes hesitation seem heroic, withdrawal an attack, constant changing of ground a forward charge:

> We should strike only when positively certain that the enemy's situation, the terrain and popular support are all in our favor and not in his. Otherwise we should rather fall back and carefully bide our time. There will always be opportunities; we should not rashly accept battle. In our first counter-campaign we originally planned to strike at Tan Tao-yuan's troops; we advanced twice but each time had to restrain ourselves and pull back, because they would not budge from their commanding position on the Yuantou heights. A few days later we sought out Chang Hui-tsan's troops, which were more vulnerable to our attack. In our second counter-campaign our army advanced to Tungku where, for the sole purpose of waiting for Wang Chin-yu's men to leave their strongpoint at Futien, we encamped close to the enemy for twenty-five days even at the risk of leakage of information; we rejected all impatient suggestions for a quick attack and finally attained our aim. In our third counter-campaign, although the storm was breaking all around us and we had made a detour of a thousand *li*, and although the enemy had discovered our plan to outflank him, we nevertheless exercised patience, turned back, changed our tactics to a breakthrough in the center, and finally fought the first battle successfully at Lientang. In our fourth counter-campaign, after our attack on Nanfeng had failed, we unhesitatingly withdrew, wheeled round to the enemy's right flank, and reassembled our forces in the area of Tungshao, whereupon we launched our great and victorious battle in southern Yihuang County. [*Strategy in China's Revolutionary War.*]

No victim, Mao. Even when conventional thinkers would call a thousand-mile retreat passive or weak, Mao sees it as a positive act—and uses active verbs, to persuade us.

YOUR LONG MARCH

Describe the way you have adjusted to a series of setbacks and failures in your life; use active verbs to make these reactions seem like victories, to make them seem positive. Talk like a fighter, not a victim. Instead of writing, "I had been cheated by the bankers, I felt, and after that, I was in a bad mood," try, "The bankers had cheated me, I felt, and I hated them."

_____

_____

_____

With active verbs, you know who's acting. But with passive ones, the author can avoid assigning blame—or praise—by leaving out the doer. Here, for instance, is a take-off on Pentagon public relations hand-outs by the author of *The Pooh Perplex:*

> Oil storage depots and staging areas were targeted in today's limited sorties. Civilian zones were carefully avoided. Heavy antiaircraft and SAM missile reaction was encountered and appropriate countermeasures were initiated. Losses of aircraft and personnel, if any, will be announced at a subsequent briefing. From preliminary evaluation of photographic data it is indicated that thirty-four hostile bicycles and three Communist water buffalo were rendered inoperable. [Frederick Crews, in *The Random House Handbook.*]

Bureaucrats avoid responsibility for their villainies by saying "It was done," and leaving out whodunit. In fact, whenever we overlook the will behind the act, we may slip into the passive. Here, for instance, Jack London describes the survivors of the San Francisco earthquake—true victims, but still active human beings who hitched themselves to their own delivery wagons to haul away their possessions.

> Before the flames, throughout the night, fled tens of thousands of homeless ones. Some were wrapped in blankets. Others carried bundles of bedding and dear household treasures. Sometimes a whole family was harnessed to a carriage or delivery wagon that was weighted down with their possessions. Baby buggies, toy wagons, and go-carts were used as trucks, while every other person was dragging a trunk. Yet everybody was gracious. The most perfect courtesy obtained. Never, in all San Francisco's history, were her people so kind and courteous as on this night of terror. [Jack London, in *Colliers.*]

Who weighted those wagons with possessions? Who harnessed themselves to the wagons? Who used baby buggies as trucks? If London had written these sentences with active verbs, he would have had to face the fact that these survivors fought to save themselves and their belongings. Because they took responsibility for themselves, they were not utterly victims.

ACTIVATING THE SURVIVORS

Rewrite the London passage with active verbs. You may rearrange the order, and invent whole episodes to show what London summarizes in his passive way.

_____

_____

_____

_____

WHO DID IT?

Using active verbs, rewrite the following passage to show who did what.

> About a hundred German tents were looted and fired by the Roman legion-naires, who were more violent than usual, because some of their scouts had earlier been ambushed. Prisoners were set up on crosses and were speared. Bags were knifed open, the contents spilled. It was sunset before order was restored by the Roman commander.

_____

_____

_____

_____

_____

When you keep your scene moving through active verbs, you can afford to pause at times, and to reflect on the objects that are being moved. And after much activity, you may want to rest and summarize what state it leaves you in, or what it amounts to, in the end. So *is* is only debilitating if you overuse it, as officious people do.

Let action lend life to most of what you write. Then your moments of pure being will stand out, to receive their full appreciation. In a general rush of movement a few sentences showing what it feels like to *be* hurried along in the crowd can give us a new view. But too many passives put the reader to sleep, since he sees no one doing anything, just objects being manipulated by unseen forces, floating in a mist of being.

Here, for example, the authors of *Business Writing* write as if no one would actually be doing the writing: ideas may be arranged (by whom?), interest is captured or lost (by what?), plans exist without minds.

> *Importance.* When a number of parallel ideas are to be treated as, for example, reasons, points, proposals, or advantages, the arrangement is usually that of the most important to the least important. Thus the reader's interest is captured at the start. When the points are to lead to the conclusion, however, there is the danger that the reader's interest will be lost before the conclusion is reached. In such an instance, the ideas may be arranged climactically. Another plan is to put the conclusion (or summary of the conclusion) first, followed by the supporting data in anticlimactic order (most important point first). [Janis & Dressner, *Business Writing.*]

REWRITING BUSINESS WRITING

Rewrite the above passage, using active verbs—and a writer.

_____

_____

We do learn from direct experience, whether inside or outside our skin. At times we seem active, searching out information; at others, we are more passive, allowing news to come to us. Both modes instruct us, so ultimately the test is: how closely are we in touch with what we want to say?

Our bodies enjoy motion, rest, and direct experience, so let us have all three in your verbs. In brief,

- Prefer active verbs.
- Know and say who does what.
- Keep most verbs active.
- Reserve passive verbs for victims or equations.
- Be direct.

DIRECT ACTION

I WENT to the woods because I wished to live deliberately, to front only the essential facts of life, and see if I could not learn what it had to teach, and not, when I came to die, discover that I had not lived. I did not wish to live what was not life, living is so dear; nor did I wish to practise resignation, unless it was quite necessary. I wanted to live deep and suck out all the marrow of life, to live so sturdily and Spartan-like as to put to rout all that was not life, to cut a broad swath and shave close, to drive life into a corner, and reduce it to its lowest terms, and, if it proved to be mean, why then to get the whole and genuine meanness out of it, and publish its meanness to the world: or if it were sublime, to know it by experience, and be able to give a true account of it in my next excursion. [Henry David Thoreau, *Walden.*]

WAS his trouble amnesia, then? Were they treating him for that? Was all this world normal and natural, while the world he thought he remembered was only the fantasy of an amnesic brain?

And they never let him step out of the room, not even into the corridor. Was he a prisoner, then? Had he committed a crime?

There never can be a man so lost as one who is lost in the vast and intricate corridors of his own lonely mind, where none may reach and none may save.

There never was a man so helpless as one who cannot remember. [Isaac Asimov, *Pebble in the Sky*.]

I TOLD him we were on our way home from Troy, and begged him in heaven's name to do us no hurt; but as soon as I had answered his question he gripped up two of my men, dashed them on the ground, and ate them raw, blood, bones and bowels, like a savage lion of the wilderness. Then he lay down on the ground of the cave and went to sleep: on which I should have crept up to him and plunged my sword into his heart while he was sleeping had I not known that if I did we should never be able to shift the stone. So we waited till dawn should come.

When day broke the monster again lit his fire, milked his ewes all orderly and gave each one her own young. Then he gripped up two more of my men, and as soon as he had eaten them he rolled the stone from the mouth of the cave, drove out his sheep, and put the stone back again. He had, however, left a large and long piece of olive wood in the cave, and when he had gone I and my men sharpened this at one end, and hid it in the sheep dung of which there was much in the cave. In the evening, he returned, milked his ewes, and ate two more men; whereon I went up to him with the skin of wondrous wine that Maron had given me and gave him a bowl full of it. He asked for another, and then another, so I gave them to him, and he was so much delighted that he inquired my name and I said it was "No Man."

The wine now began to take effect, and in a short time he fell dead drunk upon the ground. Then my men and I put the sharp end of the piece of olive wood in the fire till it was well burning, and drove it into the wretch's eye, turning it round and round as though it were an auger. After a while he plucked it out, flung it from him, and began crying to his neighbors for help. When they came, they said, "What ails you? Who is harming you?" and he answered, "No man is harming me." They then said that he must be ill, and had better pray to his father Neptune; so they went away, and I laughed at the success of my stratagem.

Then I hid my men by binding them under the sheep's bellies. The Cyclops, whose name was Polyphemus, groped his way to the stone, rolled it away, and sat at the mouth of the cave feeling the sheep's backs as they went out; but the men were under their bellies so he did not find one of them. Nor yet did he discover me, for I was ensconced in the thick belly-fleece of a ram which by some chance he had brought in with the ewes. But he was near finding me, for the ram went last, and he kept it for a while and talked to it.

When we were outside, I dropped from under the ram and unbound my companions. We drove the ewes down to my ship, got them on board and rowed out to sea. When we were a little way out I jeered at the Cyclops, whereon he tore up a great rock and hurled it after us; it fell in front of the ship and all but hit the rudder; the wash, moreover, that it made nearly carried us back to the land, but I kept the ship off it with a pole. [Samuel Butler, *The Story of the Odyssey*.]

23rd DAY

Variety

If you write one sentence after another the same way, we may suspect you are bored, deaf, or stupid. Repeating the *format* makes each item you talk about seem of equal value: nothing stands out. Without emphasis, your writing becomes monotonous. And monotony suggests a machine at work behind the writing: perhaps a bureaucracy, grinding out form letters, perhaps just a mechanical mind, fitting all impressions, no matter how different, into the same formula.

With variety you surprise us. You throw the spotlight on important ideas. You can put in a passive verb after a series of active ones to change the mood and prepare us to reflect on what the action means. Similarly, in a paragraph built out of nouns and verbs, you can add one adjective to soften or color the scene.

Variety keeps us off-balance, alert, expectant. It makes your writing as unpredictable and as sensitive as your heart. Variety of form suggests your mind expands and contracts with the heat of life—tenses, relaxes, focuses, goes fuzzy, swings from thought to act.

Variety used for its own sake, however, will make your writing seem as false as repetitive writing does. It will end up as artificial as this, by Daniel Defoe:

> How it came thither I knew not, nor could I in the least imagine; but, after innumerable fluttering thoughts, like a man perfectly confused, and out of myself, I came home to my fortification, not feeling, as we say, the ground I went on, but terrified to the last degree, looking behind me at every two or three steps, mistaking every bush and tree, and fancying every stump at a distance to be a man. Nor is it possible to describe how many various shapes my affrighted imagination represented things to me in, how many wild ideas were found every moment in my fancy, and what strange unaccountable whimsies came into my thoughts by the way. [*Robinson Crusoe*]

Defoe says he's confused five different ways, he's scared four ways, imagining things six ways. He admits it is not possible to describe what went on in his mind—and proves that nothing did. He has spent his energy saying more or less the same thing some dozen different ways—a triumph of variation on a theme—but, as an author, Defoe has not once sat down and thought through what one of those moments was like, and what Robinson Crusoe actually felt when he looked at one particular bush. The life is missing; the fiction apparent.

152

So let variety come naturally, as your subject grows or your attitude changes. Learn to hear your own prose, and you'll recognize if it's breathing, rising and falling with the subject—or not. If you notice your sentences all beginning with "He did," or settling into the same bump-a-dump rhythm, it's time to break the pattern. Mechanical activity can never raise consciousness—or improve prose. With that warning, then, we can look at some ways to shake up the metronome.

If you find you have written a series of short sentences in the same general form (he did not . . . he did not . . . he did not . . .) you might expand on your next thought, refining on it, lengthening your sentence. For instance, when William Faulkner describes his character stopping in fear, he uses two brief sentences saying what the boy did not hear, then a longer one saying what he did hear, and how that stopped, and what he sensed as a result. Then in three sentences, Faulkner tells us that the boy did not see the bear, did not know where it was, did not move. Of these three, the second sentence is longer than the first, and the last is the longest of all. Why? What was Faulkner focusing on here? Perhaps he was deepening our sense of the boy's fear—showing us how fast his mind raced, while his body froze:

> He heard no dogs at all. He never did hear them. He only heard the drumming of the woodpecker stop short off and knew that the bear was looking at him. He never saw it. He did not know whether it was in front of him or behind him. He did not move, holding the useless gun, which he had not even had warning to cock and which even now he did not cock, tasting in his saliva that taint as of brass which he knew now because he had smelled it when he peered under the kitchen at the huddled dogs. ["The Bear," *Collected Stories*.]

That last moment, then, grows huge, because Faulkner has established the rhythm before, in his series of terse negatives. Against the background of sentences short as a heartbeat, he has set a deep awareness. He implies the boy thought all that in one pulse.

DARK SHADOWS

Describe a frightening encounter in the dark. Use a half dozen short sentences, and one or two well-placed long sentences to echo the experience.

To make us sit up and listen, you might combine a few sentences. (After he went to X, he went to Y.) You could use words like *after, when, because, wherever,* to start clauses that absorb one or another of your sentences. *Which, that, who,* can blend in another. *Although, while,* or *but* can sop up another. So if you feel you're writing too many telegrams, get complicated—spawn subordinate clauses.

Clarence Darrow, a lawyer, habitually spoke in short, clear sentences, but when he explained to a group of prisoners why he thought they were in jail, he began to mix in some clauses beginning with *whether, because, who, that, but* and *if.* Watch for the short sentences, like the bass section—then the more complex sentences, in which his logic and anger crescendo.

> Most of all our criminal code consists in offenses against property. People are sent to jail because they have committed a crime against property. It is of very little consequence whether one hundred people more or less go to jail who ought not to go—you must protect property, because in this world property is of more importance than anything else.
>
> How is it done? These people who have property fix it so they can protect what they have. When somebody commits a crime it does not follow that he has done something that is morally wrong. The man on the outside who has committed no crime may have done something. For instance: to take all the coal in the United States and raise the price two dollars or three dollars when there is no need of it, and thus kill thousands of babies and send thousands of people to the poorhouse and tens of thousands to jail, as is done every year in the United States—this is a greater crime than all the people in our jails ever committed, but the law does not punish it. Why? Because the fellows who control the earth make the laws. If you and I had the making of the laws, the first thing we would do would be to punish the fellow who gets control of the earth. Nature put this coal in the ground for me as well as for them, and then the great railroad companies came along and fenced it up. ["Speech on Crime and Criminals."]

Ordinarily in English sentences the subject and verb—the kernel of the idea—come early. But you can leave them for last. Shifting their position, from sentence to sentence, lets you speed up the pace, then slow it down. Often you can create a feeling of suspense by putting off the point within one sentence, forcing the reader to guess and wait.

> When he first saw Hawaii, tilted below one wing of his plane, when he caught the light that comes up through the water, when he saw dry black old Diamond Head, rimmed with the tan fan of its brief beaches, he felt his heart pause. Five seconds the picture held. Then the plane righted itself, and he smelled the stale air again. He yanked his seat up.

DRINKING AND WRITING

When are you ready to write? Have a drink, and postpone your subject and verb in a few sentences that describe what you do before you actually get down to writing:

_____

_____

_____

_____

_____

_____

Because variety is infinite, I will not itemize the techniques. You get the idea. But let me remind you that the more strategies you learn, the more varied your prose becomes—one sentence concrete, the next abstract, one conversational, another more formal, one attacking, another forgiving, still another defining. Or you can stop drawing parallels: try contrasts. Mix in an occasional adjective or passive verb. You can jolt the clickety-clack of regular statements with a sudden exclamation! And what about rhetorical questions? (I break in to alert you to the next chapter.)

But do not force variations on a helpless idea. Let subtle variations of form reflect your changing view of the subject. Remember your aim: to keep the topic on fire, and the reader alert.

So, from sentence to sentence . . .

- Be brief, then go long.
- Expand and contract.
- Delay and then rush on.
- Try new beginnings.
- Add or subtract clauses.
- Postpone subject and verb—then deliver.

EXAMPLES OF VARIETY

NO land with an unvarying climate can be very beautiful. The tropics are not, for all the sentiment that is wasted on them. They seem beautiful at first, but sameness impairs the charm by and by. *Change* is the handmaiden Nature requires to do her miracles with. The land that has four well-defined seasons cannot lack beauty, or pall with monotony. Each season brings a world of enjoyment and interest in the watching of its unfolding, its gradual harmonious development, its culminating graces—and just as one begins to tire of it, it passes away and a radical change comes, with new witcheries and new glories in its train. And I think that to one in sympathy with nature, each season, in its turn, seems the loveliest. [Mark Twain, *Roughing It.*]

A FOOLISH consistency is the hobgoblin of little minds, adored by little statesmen and philosophers and divines. With consistency a great soul has simply nothing to do. He may as well concern himself with his shadow on the wall. Speak what you think now in hard words and tomorrow speak what tomorrow thinks in hard words again, though it contradict everything you said today— "Ah, so you shall be sure to be misunderstood?"—Is it so bad, then, to be misunderstood? Pythagoras was misunderstood, and Socrates, and Jesus, and Luther, and Copernicus, and Galileo, and Newton, and every pure and wise spirit that ever took flesh. To be great is to be misunderstood. [Ralph Waldo Emerson, "Self-Reliance."]

24th DAY

Posing Rhetorical Questions

Putting in an occasional question can give your prose variety and drama. A sharp question can help you attack nonsense—or defend your own argument against a potential challenge. By clarifying the problem you propose to solve, it can set up a paragraph, a chapter, a whole book. And even before you go into your answer, a well-phrased rhetorical question encourages the audience to answer it your way.

Questions undermine the authority of flat statements. If you suspect that the conventional wisdom in your field is silly, quote it, and then ask why. Here Elaine Morgan calls most evolution theorists "Tarzanists":

> A lot of Tarzanists privately realize that their explanations of bipedalism and weapon-wielding won't hold water. They have invented the doctrine of "feedback," which states that though these two theories are separately and individually nonsense, together they will just get by. It is alleged that the ape's bipedal gait, however unsteady, made him a better rock thrower (why?) and his rock throwing, however inaccurate, made him a better biped. (Why?) Eimerl and de Vore again put the awkward question: Since chimps can both walk erect and manipulate simple tools, "Why was it only the hominids who benefited from the feedback?" You may well ask.
>
> Next question: Why did the naked ape become naked? [*The Descent of Woman.*]

The questions break in, a second voice rising to challenge the theorists. Her *whys* help Morgan break us loose from our too easy belief in the experts. The *whys* help her turn the argument her way.

When we hear a question, we think of an answer—often the one the author subtly suggests. If we had heard it stated directly, we might disagree, but when we just hear a question, we say the implied answer under our breath, and we may convince ourselves.

Thus, a rhetorical question can slash your opponent, while making your friends nod in agreement with you. Imagine being a tribesman of Chief Charlot, in 1876:

> Yes, my people, the white man wants us to pay him. He comes in this intent, and says we must pay him—pay him for our own, for the things we have from

our God and our forefathers; for things he never owned and never gave us. What law or right is that? What shame or what charity? The Indian says that a woman is more shameless than a man; but the white man has less shame than our women. Since our forefathers first beheld him, more than seven times ten winters have snowed and melted. Most of them like those snows have dissolved away. Their spirits went whither they came; his, they say, go there too. Do they meet and see us here? Can he blush before his maker, or is he forever dead? Is his prayer his promise—a trust of the wind? Is it a sound without sense? . . .

Did he not feast us with our own cattle, on our own land—yes, on our plain by the cold spring? Did he not invite our hands to his papers? Did he not promise before the Sun and before the Eye that put fire in it, and in the name of both, and in the name of his own Chief—promise us what he promised: to give us what he has not given, to do what he knew he would never do? Now, because he lied, and because he yet lies, without friendship, manhood, justice, or charity, he wants us to give him money, pay him more. When shall he be satisfied? [Reported in *The Weekly Missoulian*, Montana, April 26, 1876.]

EMBARRASS YOUR OPPONENT

Imagine you are talking to someone alive or dead, whom you dislike. Challenge that person with a string of hard questions:

_____

_____

_____

_____

_____

_____

If what you write might arouse a reader to ask *you* a few hostile questions, anticipate him. Take time to ask them—and answer them your way. Then the reader may concede you are right, or, if not, he will at least feel you have considered his point of view.

Even if you don't feel your readers will disagree, they may still feel puzzled. They may notice that you seem to be contradicting yourself, or denying what folk wisdom tells us. The readers may not actually know what bothers them, but if you articulate these questions, you relieve their uncertainty—and you give yourself a chance to respond before accumulating doubts make the readers stop listening.

INSTANT SOLUTION

Take some pet idea you have, your instant solution to some current crisis at home or abroad. State it simply; then, using rhetorical questions, answer the doubts your listeners might have.

_____

_____

_____

_____

_____

_____

Thomas Wolfe began his book-length description of the way he wrote a novel by asking the questions he himself suffered under before getting down to work. Here, then, is the problem he will solve in the rest of his story:

> ... Now I was faced with another fundamental problem which every young writer must meet squarely, if he is to continue. How is a man to get his writing done? How long should he work at writing? And how often? What kind of method, if any, must he find in following his work? [*The Story of a Novel.*]

Thus, these not-yet-answered questions let us guess what topics Wolfe will cover—and what passions stir him. The questions set up a problem which the rest of his piece will solve.

A question mark may hook our curiosity at the top, but it is punctuated in part like an exclamation point. And it may suggest an outcry:

> Who can wonder at him, or do anything but pity him? Was he not head master of Roughborough School? To whom had he owed money at any time? Whose ox had he taken, whose ass had he taken, or whom had he defrauded? What whisper had ever been breathed against his moral character? If he had become rich it was by the most honorable of all means—his literary attainments; over and above his great works of scholarship, his *Meditations upon the Epistle and Character of St Jude* had placed him among the most popular of English theologians; it was so exhaustive that no one who bought it need ever meditate upon the subject again—indeed, it exhausted all who had anything to do with it. [Samuel Butler, *The Way of All Flesh.*]

In a more Western style, Mark Twain thanks heaven for juries:

> On the inquest it was shown that Buck Fanshaw, in the delirium of a wasting typhoid fever, had taken arsenic, shot himself through the body, cut his throat, and jumped out of a four-story window and broken his neck—and after due deliberation, the jury, sad and tearful, but with intelligence unblinded by its sorrow, brought in a verdict of death "by the visitation of God." What could the world do without juries? [*Roughing It.*]

SWEET OR SOUR

Use one rhetorical question at the beginning or end of a paragraph of complaints, to express your real feeling of outrage, comic or not:

_____

_____

_____

_____

What's a quick question good for?
- Attacking weak logic.
- Turning your reader's doubts to your advantage.
- Making the reader answer it your way.
- Organizing what's to come.
- Setting an emotional tone.

And how do you do it? Ask . . .
- What the reader might ask next.
- What your opponent doesn't want asked.
- What you're about to answer.

QUESTIONING EXAMPLES

I THINK I am a whig; but others say there are no whigs, and that I am an abolitionist . . . I now do no more than oppose the *extension* of slavery. I am not a Know-Nothing. That is certain. How could I be? How can any one who abhors the oppression of negroes, be in favor of degrading classes of white people? Our progress in degeneracy appears to me to be pretty rapid. As a nation, we began by declaring *"all men are created equal."* We now practically read it *"all men are created equal, except negroes."* When the Know-Nothings get control, it will read "all men are created equal, except negroes, *and foreigners, and Catholics."* When it comes to this I should prefer emigrating to some country where they make no pretence of loving liberty—to Russia, for instance, where despotism can be taken pure, and without the base alloy of hypocrisy. [Abe Lincoln.]

HOW can society ask a man to have respect for law and order when society itself does not have enough respect to treat the law enforcement officer justly? Society gives its nigger, the cop, less rights than it gives the Negro. The Negro has the constitutional right to demonstrate his just grievances. But the cop better not be caught demonstrating! Society frowns on the cop demonstrating for a salary increase, for example, even though his pay is bad. When the top-level politicians want a salary increase they have no difficulty getting it. Salaries are determined behind the closed doors of budget meetings. The cop cannot determine his salary in a secret meeting in the precinct house. [Dick Gregory, *The Shadow that Scares Me.*]

PERMIT me, therefore, to fortify this old dogma of mine somewhat. Taste is not only a part and an index of morality—it is the *only* morality. The first and last and closest trial question to any living creature is, "What do you like?" Tell me what you like, and I'll tell you what you are. Go out into the street, and ask the first man or woman you meet, what their "taste" is; and if they answer candidly, you know them, body and soul. "You, my friend in the rags, with the unsteady gait, what do *you* like?" "A pipe, and a quartern of gin." I know you. "You, good woman, with the quick step and tidy bonnet, what do you like?" "A swept hearth, and a clean tea-table; and my husband opposite me, and a baby at my breast." Good, I know you also. "You, little girl with the golden hair and the soft eyes, what do you like?" "My canary, and a run among the wood hyacinths." "You, little boy with the dirty hands, and the low forehead, what do you like?" "A shy at the sparrows, and a game at pitch farthing." Good; we know them all now. What more need we ask? [John Ruskin, "Of Taste."]

25th DAY

No Apologies

If you suspect your audience will disapprove of you, you may feel like apologizing. Don't. Audiences respect and want aggression. They despise an uncertain mind, and they do not find the timid entertaining for long. Those people who agree with you will feel betrayed if you end your piece by saying that, after all, perhaps you are wrong; and those people who disagree won't find that satisfying either. When you apologize—for your ignorance, your accent, your age, your education, for anything—you are assuming your audience will 1) notice it, and 2) dislike it. Your apology, then, forms a not very successful defense against expected blows.

If your audience really dislikes you, start out by admitting you know that. Saying it out loud clears the air; shows you already know something about them; displays your courage. A joke does this best: then the audience can laugh, admitting they do feel that way, but also settling down to listen to you. John Kennedy, for instance, could relax a hostile audience by saying, right off, what they secretly felt but didn't dare say to his face. When he entered Republican turf, he once said, "I want to express my great appreciation to all of you for your kindness in coming out and giving us a warm Hoosier welcome. I understand that this town suffered a misfortune this morning when the bank was robbed. I am confident that the *Indianapolis Star* will say Democrats Arrive and Bank Robbed. But we don't believe that." Or, talking to even richer Republicans, the managers of major corporations: "It would be premature to ask your support in the next election, and it would be inaccurate to thank you for it in the past." When he ran for the U.S. Senate, reporters hinted that his father's millions were helping him buy votes. So Kennedy began a speech to reporters, "I have just received the following telegram from my generous Daddy. It says: 'Dear Jack: Don't buy a single vote more than is necessary. I'll be damned if I'm going to pay for a landslide."

By acknowledging their suspicions, and turning them into a joke, he defused the issue, put it in perspective. Similarly when he appointed his campaign manager, Robert Kennedy, to the position that had traditionally gone to campaign managers, the press complained that his brother had no legal experience. Jack's reply: "I see nothing wrong with giving Robert some legal experience as Attor-

162

ney General before he goes out to practice law." No elaborate pretences, no serious apologies—instead, a rough admission that he knew the complaints, and was going to appoint Bobby anyway. So if you sense hostility, acknowledge it right off, but don't apologize.

POLITICAL EXERCISE

Imagine you are about to speak to a group of people in your own field; imagine, too, that they disapprove of you for some reason. Now, instead of backing down on that issue, make a joke of their suspicions—confess, or at least say what you imagine they think of you.

_____

_____

If you think you are significantly less competent than someone else the audience has heard, you could make the situation worse by saying you're sorry. Instead, turn the supposed incompetence to your advantage; boast of it. For instance, when Socrates was attacked by a series of very fancy talkers, he made a point of the difference between his way of talking and theirs. He could only speak the truth: but they knew rhetoric.

> How you, O Athenians, have been affected by my accusers, I cannot tell; but I know that they almost made me forget who I was—so persuasively did they speak; and yet they have hardly uttered a word of truth. But of the many falsehoods told by them, there was one which quite amazed me;—I mean when they said that you should be upon your guard and not allow yourselves to be deceived by the force of my eloquence. To say this, when they were certain to be detected as soon as I opened my lips and proved myself to be anything but a great speaker, did indeed appear to me most shameless—unless by the force of eloquence they mean the force of truth; for if such is their meaning, I admit that I am eloquent. [_The Dialogues of Plato_, trans. Benjamin Jowett.]

VIRTUOUS YOU

Think of something you cannot do well—math, spelling, chemistry, whatever—and imagine you are about to address a convention of people who are experts in that area. Like Socrates, don't apologize for your inability: show how it makes you valuable to them, and, perhaps, virtuous.

_____

_____

_____

_____

If you cannot bring yourself to admit the audience's hostility toward you in a joke or a statement, if you see no way to turn your disadvantage into a benefit, then you may face hard work. If the fault can be remedied by effort, perhaps you should just correct it. But perhaps the whole point, really, of what you are saying, is that you *are* wrong and they are right; if so, rearrange the order of your entire essay to prove that. But if you feel, somehow, that you may lose against a united, powerful, and vicious crowd, why bother to say you're sorry? What do you have to lose, by being bold? That seems to be the way the American patriot, Patrick Henry, felt when he urged his neighbors on to revolution, "Give me liberty, or give me death." He may have sounded a bit overwrought, but he knew that if they did not fight, he and everyone else in the room might face death as traitors before the king's firing squads. Why *not* fight?

Often, if you do not face an audience's potential hostility in a joke or a plea like Socrates', your feelings may slip into your tone, making you sound uncertain and indefinite. "It may be," you say, "I think . . . it seems." Mark Twain learned early not to drift into this vaguely apologetic tone when he went to work for a frontier newspaper:

> I asked the chief editor and proprietor (Mr. Goodman, I will call him, since it describes him as well as any name could do) for some instructions with regard to my duties, and he told me to go all over town and ask all sorts of people all sorts of questions, make notes of the information gained, and write them out for publication. And he added:
> "Never say 'We learn' so-and-so, or 'It is reported,' or 'It is rumored,' or 'We understand' so-and-so, but go to headquarters and get the absolute facts and then speak out and say 'It *is* so-and-so.' Otherwise, people will not put confidence in your news. Unassailable certainty is the thing that gives a newspaper the firmest and most valuable reputation." [*Roughing It.*]

COWBOYS AND INDIANS

Suppose you are reporting on some incident in which the whites kill a band of Indians. Remember the movies. The first time, write it as if you felt guilty for what happened, uncertain of exactly how it happened, confused about who to blame. The second time, take a pro-white view, cutting out all doubt. The third time, ask yourself what you really think went on, but write it without any *probablys* or *perhapses:* your view, *as if* you knew for sure.

1. _____
_____
_____
_____
_____

2. _____
_____
_____
_____
_____

3. _____

_____

_____

_____

_____

We have been trained to be polite. We know better than to say an angry word, and if we think someone else is angry at us, we've been taught not to provoke them. But we can be courteous while bringing that conflict out into the open, to be discussed. It may disarm the audience; it may turn out to be an argument in our behalf; it may simply be a refusal to deny our own anger. But in any case, such expression will keep us from turning mealy-mouthed. When the British had almost sunk his ship, they asked John Paul Jones if he would surrender. "I have not yet begun to fight." That's the spirit.

MORE NON-APOLOGIZERS

IF you're so concerned with what you call my personal artistic integrity, you don't belong in the picture business. [Producer David O. Selznick.]

WHEN he was attacked for soaring over budget making *The Ten Commandments*, Cecil B. DeMille replied: "What do they want me to do? Stop now—and release it as *The Five Commandments?*"

THE trouble with censors is they worry if a woman has cleavage. They ought to worry if she hasn't any. [Marilyn Monroe.]

I NOW had a vast quantity of paper at my disposal, and I set about filling the notebooks with odd facts, stories from the past, and all sorts of other things, often including the most trivial material. On the whole I concentrated on things and people that I found charming and splendid; my notes are also full of poems and observations on trees and plants, birds and insects. I was sure that when people saw my book they would say, "It's even worse than I expected. Now one can really tell what she is like." After all, it is written entirely for my own amusement and I put things down exactly as they came to me. How could my casual jottings possibly bear comparison with the many impressive books that exist in our time? Readers have declared, however, that I can be proud of my work. This has surprised me greatly; yet I suppose it is not so strange that people should like it, for, as will be gathered from these notes of mine, I am the sort of person who approves of what others abhor and detests the things they like. [Sei Shonagon, *The Pillow Book of Sei Shonagon*, trans. Ivan Morris.]

26th DAY

Summing Up

After many words, few—boiling your whole essay down into a sentence, distilling your information to its essence, then hardening that into one image. That is summing up.

In a phrase, or at most a paragraph, the adroit summary refers back to each key idea you discuss in the larger piece, connects them to your main point, and stops. Brevity—not expansive geniality—makes a summary useful.

By reducing a long argument to its essential phrases, you help the reader see the central thought, separated from its proofs. And that, in turn, helps her remember it.

Like a net, the summary can be flung wide, to catch a whole school of minnowy details, then drawn tight, squeezing out the water, and leaving us with the generalization, "That's all fish." Emerson says, "To believe your own thought, to believe that what is true for you in your private heart is true for all men—that is genius." *That* snares two beliefs, each complex, then delivers both to genius. So Emerson has thrown his net around a lot of thought, then shrunk it from twenty-five to three words.

To be accurate, a summary should carry the scent of the rest of what you have written. Catch the emotions you've been experiencing over the last few pages—pull them loose from the scenery, as Mark Twain does:

> And it was comfort in those succeeding days to sit up and contemplate the majestic panorama of mountains and valleys spread out below us and eat ham and hard boiled eggs while our spiritual natures revelled alternately in rainbows, thunderstorms, and peerless sunsets. Nothing helps scenery like ham and eggs. [*Roughing It.*]

We can hear his satisfaction and his honesty. Ham and eggs do improve our appreciation of nature: but how much duller that idea could have become if Twain had not had the wit to be brief.

Again, if you have been offering the reader one picture after another, reach for a visual summary—an image or a story through which we can combine the various items you've put before our mind's eye into one landscape. When Mark Twain had traveled by stage coach for nineteen days, through hundreds of miles of shrubs, desert, and wasteland, he described what he felt and saw on the nineteenth day, pausing at the end to survey the whole:

> On the nineteenth day we crossed the Great American Desert—forty memorable miles of bottomless sand, into which the coach wheels sunk from six inches to a foot. We worked our passage most of the way across. That is to say, we got out and walked. It was a dreary pull and a long and thirsty one, for we had no water. From one extremity of this desert to the other, the road was white with the bones of oxen and horses. It would hardly be an exaggeration to say that we could have walked the forty miles and set our feet on a bone at every step! The desert was one prodigious graveyard.

We can almost see that. The word *graveyard* recalls the bones at every step, but more, it reminds us of the dreariness, the depression, the desolation he has been emphasizing for pages before. And directly after this sentence, he adds to the bones: "And the log-chains, wagon tyres and rotting wrecks of vehicles were almost as thick as the bones." And so he proceeds to lament the amount of suffering the first pioneers endured.

You can summarize at the beginning, end, or middle of your piece—anywhere you feel the need to draw together a wide experience into a half-dozen words. Eldridge Cleaver, for instance, reflects at length on the way he lost his self-respect when he went to prison. Then he pivots, to show us how that led him to write. (The pivot, here, sums up the first paragraph, and tilts into the third.)

> After I returned to prison, I took a long look at myself and, for the first time in my life, admitted that I was wrong, that I had gone astray—astray not so much from the white man's law as from being human, civilized—for I could not approve the act of rape. Even though I had some insight into my own motivations, I did not feel justified. I lost my self-respect. My pride as a man dissolved and my whole fragile moral structure seemed to collapse, completely shattered.
> That is why I started to write. To save myself.
> I realized that no one could save me but myself. The prison authorities were both uninterested and unable to help me. I had to seek out the truth and unravel the snarled web of my motivations. I had to find out who I am and what I want to be, what type of man I should be, and what I could do to become the best of which I was capable. I understood that what had happened to me had also happened to countless other blacks and it would happen to many, many more. [*Soul on Ice.*]

WHAT'S THE POINT?

1. In three or five words, sum up the point of three paragraphs you have written in the chapters "Humanizing" and "Being Conversational."

---

2. Imagine pivoting from some other paragraph to another topic, by summing up the first, then hinting at the next:

When you've thought of a phrase or a sentence that does sum up your ideas, your feelings, and your images, you will probably feel the need to distinguish it from the rest of your comments.

How do you signal that the summary is important? By an abrupt change of expected rhythm or texture. After long rambling sentences, try two words. After meandering arguments over the definitions of words, call on a single image. Or expand to one generalization after having noted a thousand details. By breaking with a pattern the reader has been lulled into expecting, you set off your summary, draw attention to it, *italicize*. Here, for instance, John Hersey describes the first effects of the atom bomb dropped on Hiroshima:

> Everything fell, and Miss Sasaki lost consciousness. The ceiling dropped suddenly and the wooden floor above collapsed in splinters and the people up there came down and the roof above them gave way; but principally and first of all, the bookcases right behind her swooped forward and the contents threw her down, with the left leg horribly twisted and breaking underneath her. There, in the tin factory, in the first moment of the atomic age, a human being was crushed by books. [*Hiroshima*.]

The bulk of the paragraph falls forward: we see, we wince as we feel, we can hear everything tumble onto Miss Sasaki. Then Hersey slows the pace, and switches from the particular tragedy to sum it up in the ironic perspective of history.

And when Norman Mailer described the prize fight in which Griffith killed Paret in the twelfth round, he focused first on the way Griffith whaled into the Cuban on the ropes, and Mailer's sentences repeat the same view, the same tone over and over. Then he shifts to Paret. And in five words, he sums up the fight: its literal truth. Having made that change of focus, he can expatiate on the death in slow motion, recalling it, then summing up that impression of echoing punches in a final image:

> I was sitting in the second row of that corner—they were not ten feet away from me, and like everybody else, I was hypnotized. I had never seen one man hit another so hard and so many times. Over the referee's face came a look of woe as if some spasm had passed its way through him, and then he leaped on Griffith to pull him away. It was the act of a brave man. Griffith was uncontrollable. His trainer leaped into the ring, his manager, his cut man, there were four people holding Griffith, but he was off on an orgy, he had left the Garden, he was back on a hoodlum's street. If he had been able to break loose from his handlers and the referee, he would have jumped Paret to the floor and whaled on him there.
>
> And Paret? Paret died on his feet. As he took those eighteen punches something happened to everyone who was in psychic range of the event. Some part of his death reached out to us. One felt it hover in the air. He was still standing in the ropes, trapped as he had been before, he gave some little half-smile of regret, as if he were saying, "I didn't know I was going to die just

yet," and then, his head leaning back but still erect, his death came to breathe about him. He began to pass away. As he passed, so his limbs descended beneath him, and he sank slowly to the floor. He went down more slowly than any fighter had ever gone down, he went down like a large ship which turns on end and slides second by second into its grave. As he went down, the sound of Griffith's punches echoed in the mind like a heavy ax in the distance, chopping into a wet log. [*The Presidential Papers.*]

EPITAPH

Using long sentences, describe someone dying slowly; then, somewhere in that paragraph, use one short sentence to sum up the way that person died.

If most of a paragraph has dealt with words about words, struggling toward some abstract but hard-to-define ideal, you might want to change the texture from intellectual cobwebs to imagery for your quick summary. The best images carry as many facets as a large diamond: they sparkle with multiple reflections. A single image suggests a hundred lights, countless meanings. And, as Thoreau says, the condensed statement often makes a greater impact than the more leisurely one:

> August 22, 1851 ... It is the fault of some excellent writers—De Quincey's first impressions on seeing London suggest it to me—that they express themselves with too great fullness and detail. They ... lack moderation and sententiousness. They ... say all they mean. Their sentences are not concentrated and nutty. Sentences which suggest far more than they say, which have an atmosphere about them, which do not merely report an old, but make a new impression ... to frame these, that is the *art* of writing. Sentences which are expensive, towards which so many volumes, so much life, went; which lie like boulders on the page, up and down or across; which contain the seed of other sentences, not mere repetition, but creation; which a man might sell his grounds and castles to build. If De Quincey had suggested each of his pages in a sentence and passed on, it would have been far more excellent writing. His style is nowhere kinked and knotted up into something hard and significant, which you could swallow like a diamond, without digesting. [In H.S. Canby, *Thoreau.*]

MY LOCAL PAPER

What does your local newspaper look like? Without using imagery, describe the headlines, photos, editorials, features it has. Then shift to a single strong image, to sum up.

When you recognize the way you have been writing, you will see how to write your summary—differently. But whether you decide to switch to an image, a general idea, a shocking phrase, or a sudden simplicity, you will need to condense much into little: somehow, your summary must take a fraction of the space, while suggesting or recalling . . .

- Visual highlights.
- Emotional overtones.
- Each main point.

Summing up resembles writing a one-line poem.

STRONG SUMMARIES

Now you see, you don't do this thing a bit better than you did a fortnight ago; and I'll tell you the reason. You want to learn accounts; that's well and good. But you think all you need do to learn accounts is to come to me and do sums for an hour or so, two or three times a week; and no sooner do you get your caps on and turn out of doors again, than you sweep the whole thing clean out of your mind. . . . A man that had got his heart in learning figures would make sums for himself, and work 'em in his head: when he sat at his shoemaking he'd count his stitches by fives, and then put a price on his stitches, say half a farthing, and then see how much money he could get in an hour; and then ask himself how much money he'd get in a day at that rate; and then how much ten workmen would get working three, or twenty, or a hundred years at that rate—and all the while his needle would be going just as fast as if he left his head empty for the devil to dance in. But the long and the short of it is—I'll have nobody in my night school that doesn't strive to learn what he comes to learn, as hard as if he was striving to get out of a dark hole into broad daylight. I'll send no man away because he's stupid; if Billy Taft, the idiot, wanted to learn anything, I'd not refuse to teach him. But I'll not throw away good knowledge on people who think they can get it by the sixpenn'orth, and carry it away with 'em as they would an ounce of snuff. So never come to me again, if you can't show that you've been working with your own heads, instead of thinking you can pay for mine to work for you. That's the last word I've got to say to you. [George Eliot, *Adam Bede*.]

EVERY smallest stroke of virtue or of vice leaves its never so little scar. The drunken Rip Van Winkle, in Jefferson's play, excuses himself for every fresh dereliction by saying, "I won't count this time!" Well! He may not count it, and a kind Heaven may not count it; but it is being counted nonetheless. Down among his nerve-cells and fibres the molecules are counting it, registering and storing it up to be used against him when the next temptation comes. Nothing we ever do is, in strict scientific literalness, wiped out. [William James, *Principles of Psychology*.]

27th DAY

Handling Criticism

When you write, do you hear a critic inside your head, commenting on each sentence as you finish it? If so, shoot that critic.

If you let your mind criticize your writing as you go, you may stop and brood about whether to put in a comma, or take out an idea, and never finish. Imagine your mind has guards. When an idea begins, it may seem slight, even silly. If your guards get too tough, they may bruise or kill an idea which, if left to grow, might lead to a half a dozen others. Those trigger-happy watchmen named fear and shame and obedience wreck more ideas than stupidity ever could.

So withdraw the watchers from the gate as you work. How? Write a few pages of whatever comes into your mind; daydream freely, then take notes; listen for the first peep out of that critic, and then imagine strangling him. You may find some help sidestepping the internal critic by drinking bourbon, like the novelist William Faulkner, or by taking opium, like the poets Baudelaire and Coleridge. But using such stimulants tends to bloat your prose style: Faulkner's ramble and Coleridge's dreamy swoon seem, in part, to derive from their intoxication.

Critics should wait until you've finished your first draft, the huge, rough, uneven pouring out of thoughts, some almost polished, some incomplete. Even better, keep the critics away until you've revised that and have typed it up, made it look near-perfect.

Even then, postpone releasing your old enemy, the internal critic. What you need most is a neutral outside observer who can answer some of your questions objectively. Not friends. Not relatives. Not lovers. (They will encourage or discourage you for reasons that have little to do with your writing.) Who, then? Ideally, an editor, or another writer: someone who has a professional interest in writing.

Be clear in your own mind that you are asking for advice. Recognize that you probably want everyone to think what you've written is wonderful. Deep down, you may not want objective criticism, even if it is friendly. And that unwillingness to hear your baby criticized may keep you from understanding the suggestions or following them.

If you notice resentment rising, ask yourself: is this critic, basically, friendly or not? Does he seem aware of my aims? Is he sympathetic to them? In general,

172

does he seem objective? If so, listen harder; he's probably friendly, and you're probably just balking to protect your cherished creation. But if you sense the comments getting too picky, if you feel the person is actually rewriting what you've done, or changing your ideas, that's unfriendly: forget him, and don't take that advice.

When you hand your manuscript over to an editor or to another writer, you may want more than praise: having suffered over each paragraph, your mind may also want to quibble over each phrase or sentence, or the placement of every section. But put that little stuff off. Try, at first, to focus on the larger picture. When you know the *general* impression your piece makes, then you can figure out what direction to go in for particular, small, even petty changes. Having been down cutting a path through the jungle, you cannot know what the valleys look like from the air—an observer who flies over the entire area can tell you what really stands out, what's misty, what falls away. So before you ask him to look at your woodchips, get the overview.

For a look at the whole, ask the editor:

- Is the main point clear?
- Does it seem original?
- Do any parts seem out of order?
- Are the proportions about right?
- What parts do not make sense?
- What seems repetitive?
- Is the tone appropriate to the subject,
  and to the intended audience?
- Overall, does it work?

The answers to these questions will tell you more than any suggested changes could. For instance, the editor may notice that a certain page seems muzzy, uncertain, almost silly: listen to that. That tells you the page needs work. But be leery of his specific suggestions for how to fix it. Maybe those would work, maybe not. Don't worry about the particulars of correcting so soon; just make a mental note that something needs to be cleared up there. In general, use comments as a signal that something has gone wrong; but find your own way to make it right.

An editor, then, acts as an articulate reader, one who can put a finger on the passages that puzzle or delight. But the editor cannot really act as a substitute writer. You know more about the subject; you've spent more hours filtering the information, sorting it out, rearranging it; you've solved innumerable problems that came up in expressing these ideas. You're the expert, and your mind now seems supersaturated with this material. As a result, even though a friendly critic may be able to spot a problem with your presentation, you're the only one who can patch that, then polish the whole.

In fact, you could edit yourself, if you had time enough to let the manuscript sit on your shelf for nine years, as Horace recommended. Time gives distance, but lets you forget your original data. Talking with a neutral observer helps you get that perspective, without losing the immediacy and taste of your subject.

Changing what you've written may hurt. You chop a whole section that took weeks to put together. You explain what you thought you could just hint at. You add the list you knew you needed, but left out because you'd lost your notes.

You drag a comb through your wild and scraggly prose. And throughout, resentment bubbles. How could anyone find anything to criticize in your work? Why change anything in this masterpiece? When you feel this, take a break. Daydream a bit: think of how you would torture the editor or critic. Envision that in detail. Work off some of your anger. (If you don't do something like this, the anger will remain, and swell, until you find it fills so much of your mind that you cannot even think about doing the revisions.)

The way you handle criticism will tell you whether you're more interested in short-term praise or long-term craft. If you fret and debate and hem and haw, you're probably more interested in applause than advice. But if you know, in your calmer moments, that the advice makes sense, and if you can trick your mind into letting you rework the manuscript, then you will find your ideas emerging from the rampage of sentences, your jokes getting sharper, your effects subtler. Having written the piece, you now know what you meant to say back at the beginning, and can rewrite it without difficulty. Gradually, your pride grows.

You see where you're headed, and, occasionally, you realize you're getting there. When you've digested a friendly editor's criticism and have applied it, you will find you move closer to what you originally planned.

You do not lose originality through changing; you let more shine through.

CRITICAL CHANGES

From drafts of this book:

First draft: What does your local newspaper read like?
Editor's comment: This sentence is ungrammatical and awkward.
Revised version: What does your local newspaper look like?

First draft: Now, thinking of yourself in comparison with your reader, how do you sum up your relationship?
Editor's comment: Do you mean, "Comparing yourself with your reader"? This construction is awkward.
Revised version: Now, thinking of yourself and your reader, how do you sum up your relationship?

First draft: A paragraph is a pleasant unit.
Editor's comment: *Pleasant* seems a weak word—logical, helpful?
Revised version: A paragraph is a useful unit.

M**Y** spirit quivered at the bloody execution. My soul recoiled before the carnage of so many lovely things cut out upon which my heart was set. But it had to be done, and we did it. [Thomas Wolfe, *The Story of a Novel.*]

28th DAY

Revising

Before you begin to revise, consider whether you have enough distance from the manuscript. Time gives you perspective, for instance: after a few years, you can see if the writing still lives for you, and if it does, you can spot the occasional falsities, the wrong turns, the lazy omissions. Listening to an editor or a colleague *may* give you a fresh way of looking at it. Even typing helps. The poet W. H. Auden says:

> Most people enjoy the sight of their own handwriting as they enjoy the smell of their own farts. Much as I loathe the typewriter, I must admit that it is a help in self-criticism. Typescript is so impersonal and hideous to look at that, if I type out a poem, I immediately see defects which I missed when I looked through it in manuscript. When it comes to a poem by somebody else, the severest test I know of is to write it out in longhand. The physical tedium of doing this ensures that the slightest defect will reveal itself; the hand is constantly looking for an excuse to stop. [*The Dyer's Hand.*]

Norman Mailer had lived with *The Deer Park* for three years, but he had been away from it for six months when Putnam's decided to publish it. His editor there, Ted Purdy, told him, "We like it just the way it is." But Mailer, somehow, felt he might want to revise the manuscript, after all that time away from it:

> Well, I wanted to take a look. After all, I had been learning new lessons. I began to go over the page proofs, and the book read as if it had been written by someone else. I was changed from the writer who had labored on that novel, enough to be able to see it without anger or vanity or the itch to justify myself. Now, after three years of living with the book, I could at last admit the style was wrong, that it had been wrong from the time I started, that I had been strangling the life of my novel in a poetic prose which was too self-consciously attractive and formal, false to the life of my characters, especially false to the life of my narrator who was the voice of my novel, and so gave the story its air. [*Advertisements for Myself.*]

The more distance you have from the manuscript, the easier you will find you can face the need for major changes. Mailer felt he had to redo his style throughout. You might realize that the idea you started out with has somehow veered and tacked and become its opposite by the end. Or one section pushes up like a volcano, making every other section seem like bumps on the horizon. Perhaps one part makes no sense. Only when you consider the entire work, reading through it more or less as a stranger, pretending you are meeting it for the first time, can you see the major problems and recognize the need for substantial revision.

Distance gives you courage and coldness; you begin to understand what you have created, and therefore how to improve it. You can judge the work *as if* you were an indifferent reader—and, as writer, you can then adjust each sentence for that reader's convenience:

> A man may, and ought to take pains to write clearly, tersely and euphoniously: he will write many a sentence three or four times over—to do much more than this is worse than not rewriting at all: he will be at great pains to see that he does not repeat himself, to arrange his matter in the way that shall best enable the reader to master it, to cut out superfluous words and, even more, to eschew irrelevant matter: but in each case he will be thinking not of his own style but of his reader's convenience. [Samuel Butler, *Thought and Language.*]

When looking at any whole, ask yourself: have I delivered what I promised? Kenneth Burke philosophizes about our sense of form: "A work has form in so far as one part of it leads a reader to anticipate another part, to be gratified by the sequence." When we start a work, we intend to explore X, and the reader goes forward expecting to find X. If we then turn aside, and spend forty pages on M, we may irritate or lose our reader.

PROMISES, PROMISES

Look back at some paragraph you've written earlier in this book. Does the beginning promise what the rest of the paragraph delivers? If the subject or the idea to come is not clear, rewrite the opening sentence here:

_____

_____

_____

From the top of a mountain, you can tell where a valley leads; you can trace the flow of the stream, and see its main direction despite twists and trees. Similarly, when we consider the whole piece of writing, we want to know if we have slipped too far out of our main channel. Have we, for instance, overdone some section, larding in too much data, making it too long, drawing attention away from the main line of argument? Or, in another section, have we forgotten how it fits into the general flow? These questions involve focus: have we kept our eye on the central subject, and on what we have to say about *that*? Or have we been tempted to slip away into some swamp?

When we have a strong idea of where we are headed, and in general, how we are going to get there, we gauge our pace by obstacles: does this slight curve take us closer to our goal or merely add mileage? If we solve this little problem, do we find our speed increases? Raising doubts, then resolving them, we establish a rhythm of forward motion. As one question gets answered, then, do we as readers wonder about some others, to be covered in the next chapter? Do we feel suspense draw us into the next difficulty, yearning for a satisfying finale? Does the writing lead us on?

An argument or a story should seem to unfold like a flower growing; we know what kind of bloom to expect, but from day to day we are surprised, disappointed, relieved, and perhaps astonished as we see how the petals swell and change color. As we read, do we gradually discover new ways of looking at the central subject? And is the process itself beautiful?

And what about the result? Do we end up with a real conclusion? If so, is it just one—or do we have a series of half-stops? Is the point clear? If we have posed some problem, do we offer a solution, or do we instead beg off, saying we hope for one sometime? What have we contributed to the world that the world did not know before, or see quite that way?

ANALYZING FORWARD MOTION

Look at another paragraph you have written, and diagnose it, answering these questions: 1. What is the focus of the paragraph? 2. Why would a reader want to read through it to the end? 3. What is the conclusion? Then condense, and improve the movement of that paragraph.

1. _____

2. _____

3. _____

_____

_____

_____

Once you have sharpened your focus and tested your conclusions, you will know whether or not you need to change your tone. Sometimes you may sound half-crazed at the start, then discover that your best passages are reasonable, quiet. Or, like Mailer revising *The Deer Park,* you find out that what you mean deserves a lot tougher tone than you've been using.

That's the time for word-by-word work. If you have thought hard about the larger issues, though, you will have some guidelines, rough aims by which you can gauge your smaller revisions. You begin to listen for the slight shifts in sound and pace that one syllable unsettles. At this level, you can add meaning with a stroke, and make the rhythm reinforce it. Or you can hesitate over six possible versions of one sentence, torturing yourself with uncertainty, until you give up and go on to maul some other paragraph, as Mailer did:

> An example: in the Rinehart *Deer Park* I had this: "They make Sugar sound so good in the newspapers," she declared one night to some people in a bar, "that I'll really try him. I really will, Sugar." And she gave me a sisterly kiss.

I happened to change that very little, I put in "said" instead of "declared" and later added "older sister," so that it now read:

And she gave me a sisterly kiss. Older sister.

Just two words, but I felt as if I had revealed some divine law of nature, had laid down an invaluable clue—the kiss of an older sister was a worldly universe away from the kiss of a younger sister—and I thought to give myself the Nobel Prize for having brought such illumination and *division* to the cliche of the sisterly kiss.

Well, as an addition it wasn't bad fun, and for two words it did a bit to give a sense of what was working back and forth between Sergius and Lulu, it was another small example of Sergius' hard eye for the world, and his cool sense of his place in it, and all this was to the good, or would have been for a reader who went slowly, and stopped, and thought. But if anyone was in a hurry, the little sentence "Older sister" was like a finger in the eye, it jabbed the unconscious, and gave an uncomfortable nip of rhythm to the mind.

I had five hundred changes of this kind. I started with the first paragraph of the book, on the third sentence which pokes the reader with its backed-up rhythm, "Some time ago," and I did that with intent, to slow my readers from the start, like a fighter who throws his right two seconds after the bell, and so gives the other man no chance to decide on the pace. [*Advertisements for Myself.*]

Mailer found he was improving the text one way, ruining it another; adding meaning, but balking the reader. You can sidestep that dilemma *before* you start tinkering by deciding exactly what style seems to work best with this material. In your first draft, certain passages seem to make a strong impression on you. How would you describe the style there, the tone? Style's such a fluid phenomenon that you cannot categorize it with someone else's terms: romantic, classical, or baroque. So make up your own name for that tone: a label that means a lot to you. Then figure out what the main components of *that* style are:

- What level of vocabulary?
- What length of words?
- Elaborate or simple sentences?
- Complex or easy paragraphs?
- What emotional mood?
- How dense with information and argument?
- Is the work mainly logic, story, attack, or what?
- How much imagery will you use?
- What devices of rhythm and organization?

You might flip back through the previous chapters for more detailed suggestions on style. But you must build your own: the tone that sounds right to you, for this particular subject. Which suits it better: a conversational or a logical style? A concrete narrative or a series of definitions and attacks?

At this stage, you may also find you have solved problems that vexed you as you wrote: how to describe a key person or issue, say. You have had more time to think: you have accepted, and rejected, a dozen possible ways of saying that; now, at last, seeing the whole, you perceive the image or word that says it best.

Flaubert suggested that there would always be one word that was exact, moving, and correct. In searching for this *mot juste,* you may find you turn your manuscript into a tangle of insertions, crossings out, scribbles.

(Look at your description of a person or a place in the second or third chapters, and look for soft words, vague phrases, limp passages. Then try out a number of alternative wordings, until you find *le mot juste*. Write the results down, circling your revision; then ponder the sentence's rhythm and meaning. If you do not find the result an improvement, go on tinkering to make it successful.)

The last, and least important, stage of revision takes you through spelling and grammar booboos, typos, footnote checking, smashing cliches, perhaps finding substitutes for a word you've used too often. Unfortunately school trains people to think that's all revision is: housecleaning.

But real revision comes from your revised understanding of what you've already written. When you step far enough back from the manuscript to look at it whole, you can gauge its overall shape, pace, power. With this renewed sense of what you've written—and what you really mean—you can adjust the relative size and weight of the parts so that the less important sections do not overpower the main line of your argument; you can gauge the rough rhythm and speed of the piece, seeing if it really pulls you through the material; you can test to see if your ending delivers what your beginning seems to promise; and you can define the most appropriate tone.

Revising, then, simplifies and deepens. It organizes, and strengthens the rhythm. It cuts away the unnecessary, emphasizes the important, smoothes out the movement. It reveals your deeper meaning, and silhouettes your own originality.

There is no perfect final form. You stop when you have made the writing work for you. If you imagine there is only one ideal way to write your piece, you will revise it to death. So remember John Dewey, who said, "Not perfection as the final goal, but the ever enduring process of perfecting, maturing, refining, is the aim in living." Part of maturing is also leaving well enough alone. When you've got the manuscript *almost* perfect, stop. That way you'll save your writing's natural vitality.

So give yourself time to revise with calm. And, at each level of the whole, part, paragraph, or phrase, ask yourself:

- Am I delivering what I promised?
- Have I maintained my focus on my main subject?
- Does it move?
- Do I reach a real conclusion?
- Is my tone appropriate?
- Should I stop revising now?

SOME REVISIONS

FIRST DRAFT: Miss Pontifex soon found out that Ernest did not like games—but she saw also that he could hardly be expected to like them. He was perfectly well shaped but unusually devoid of physical muscular strength. He got a fair share of this in after life, but it came much later with him than with other boys and at the time I write of he was a mere little skeleton. He wanted something to develop his arms and chest without knocking him about as much as the school games did. To supply this want was Alethea's first anxity. It seemed to her that carpentry would be about the sort of thing that would do for him, but she did not like to propose it for fear of making him think that she too was like everyone else anxious to make him do things for his good which he disliked doing.

Whatever it was to be it must be something which he should take a fancy to and like as much as other boys liked cricket or football, and it must appear to him as though the wish for it had come originally from himself; and this was not so easy to hit upon, but ere long it occurred to her that she might enlist Ernest's love of music on her side, and asked him one night he was spending a half holiday at her house whether he would like to have an organ of his own to play on. Of course the boy said yes; and then she told him about her grandfather and the organ which he had built for himself; and so fired his imagination. It had never entered into his head that he could make one, but when he gathered that from what his aunt had said that this was not out of the question, he rose as eagerly to the bait as his aunt could have desired and wanted to begin learning to saw and plane so that he might make the pipes at once.

Miss Pontifex was much pleased, she did not see how she could well have hit upon anything more suitable. Rowing would have done but there was no river at Roughborough and she liked also the idea that he would incidentally get a knowledge of carpentering, for she was impressed, perhaps foolishly, with the wisdom of the German custom which gives every boy a handicraft of some sort; but she kept this source of pleasure carefully to herself, for she was above all things anxious to avoid his thinking that she wanted him to do things that would be of use to him. Her main idea was to amuse and interest him and help him to a little more muscular development.

REVISED VERSION: Miss Pontifex soon found out that Ernest did not like games—but she saw also that he could hardly be expected to like them. He was perfectly well shaped but unusually devoid of physical muscular strength. He got a fair share of this in after life, but it came much later with him than with other boys and at the time of which I am writing he was a mere little skeleton. He wanted something to develop his arms and chest without knocking him about as much as the school games did. To supply this want by some means which should add also to his pleasures was Alethea's first anxiety. Rowing would have answered every purpose, but unfortunately there was no river at Roughborough.

Whatever it was to be it must be something which he should like as much as other boys liked cricket or football, and he must think the wish for it to have come originally from himself; it was not very easy to find anything that would do, but ere long it occurred to her that she might enlist his love of music on her side, and asked him one day when he was spending a half holiday at her house whether he would like her to buy an organ for him to play on. Of course the boy said yes; then she told him about her grandfather and the organs he had built. It had never entered into his head that he could make one, but when he gathered from what his aunt had said that this was not out of the question, he rose as eagerly to the bait as she could have desired and wanted to begin learning to saw and plane so that he might make the wooden pipes at once.

Miss Pontifex did not see how she could well have hit upon anything more suitable, and she liked also the idea that he would incidentally get a knowledge of carpentering, for she was impressed, perhaps foolishly, with the wisdom of the German custom which gives every boy a handicraft of some sort. [Samuel Butler, *The Way of All Flesh.*]

FIRST DRAFT: He went out of the house, but as his blood cooled he felt that the chief result of the discussion was a deposit of dread within him at the idea of opening with his wife in future subjects which might again urge him to violent speech. It was as if a fatal fracture had begun, and he was afraid of any movement that might make it fatal. His marriage would be a mere piece of bitter irony if they could not go on loving each other tenderly, and his inward effort after that outburst was entirely to excuse her and to blame the hard circumstances which were partly his fault. He tried to heal the wound he had made by petting her, and it was not in Rosamond's nature to be repellent or sulky; indeed she was pleased with such signs that her husband was fond of her and that she could control him. But this was something quite distinct from her loving *him.*

FINAL VERSION: He went out of the house, but as his blood cooled he felt that the chief result of the discussion was a deposit of dread within him at the idea of opening with his wife in future subjects which might again urge him to violent speech. It was as if a fracture in delicate crystal had begun, and he was afraid of any movement that might make it fatal. His marriage would be a mere piece of bitter irony if they could not go on loving each other. He had long ago made up his mind to what he thought was her negative character—her want of sensibility which showed itself in disregard both of his specific wishes and of his general aims. The first great disappointment had been borne: the tender devotedness and docile adoration of the ideal wife must be renounced, and life must be taken up on a lower stage of expectation, as it is by men who have lost their limbs. But the real wife had not only her claims, she had still a hold on his heart and it was his intense desire that the hold should remain strong. In marriage the certainty, "She will never love me much," is easier to bear than the fear "I shall love her no more." Hence after that outburst his inward effort was entirely to excuse her and to blame the hard circumstances which were partly his fault. He tried that evening by petting her to heal the wound he had made in the morning, and it was not in Rosamond's nature to be repellent or sulky; indeed, she welcomed the signs that her husband loved her and was under control. But this was something quite distinct from loving *him.* [George Eliot, *Middlemarch.*]

29th DAY

Ending

The last impression you leave a reader with may determine his judgment on your work. So be aggressive: if your article is argumentative, go for a conviction; if you lament some falling off or decay, make your last paragraphs cry out. The reader expects you to defend your assertions—more, to drive them home with force. Readers *prefer* the knockout. Weak endings do not stop, they peter out. After the last line of one of his poems, Miller Williams says, he wants the reader to go through the windshield. So let forward momentum carry the reader past the last word, into some shock of his own, some further realization.

Where the beginning raises a question, the bold end answers it—or seems to. By now you should be able to solve the crucial problems you discuss, so do so. Sum up. This reassures the reader that he has understood you correctly, and reinforces your message in his mind.

And when you take a clear position at the end, you will find you can revise your first paragraph to match. (When you began, who knew how your views would change? Now that you've found out what you really think, you can change your opening paragraphs so they reflect what the rest of your paper actually says.)

A strong ending, then, responds to the beginning: answers it, bears it out, confirms the attitude you suggested there, but deepens it, gives your views a final twist. For instance, Skip Rozin started an article on strip mining by coining a word for "killing the land," then echoed that at the end, when he talked about the results: here are his first paragraph, and his close:

> The word is terracide. As in homicide, or genocide. Except it's terra. Land.
> . . . .
> And the stripping goes on. At the current pace over 60,000 acres of Letcher County alone will be "disturbed" by strip mining by 1990, leaving less than 700 acres of farmland.
> Eighteen years from now, in 1990.
> But this is the Cumberland Plateau—Daniel Boone country.
> These are mountain people, and mountains hold a man in place. They always have. But what happens when the mountains are gone?
> The word is genocide. As in terracide. ["People of the Ruined Hills," in *The Essay*.]

By answering a question you raised at the beginning, or repeating a phrase, your ending will give a reader a sense of closure. We find out your final decision. For you may have balanced and hedged and debated throughout the earlier pages, but now we come back to the essential issue, and you have a chance to speak up. If you don't, we may feel you lack emotional commitment to your point or, worse, you have lost your sense of direction.

ENDING BEYOND WHERE YOU BEGAN

Suppose you have to write a short essay on capital punishment. Write a first paragraph setting up a problem or debate; then write a brief last paragraph, resolving the issue.

_____

_____

_____

_____

_____

_____

_____

_____

_____

_____

_____

An ending can do more than stop debate and allay suspense. To give your conclusions greater force, you may want to make your close resemble those real-life events we call decisive endings: victory, death, farewell.

Or you might have one last thought, a complete one that encompasses everything you've taken us through, yet gives it the light of final understanding, as in this essay by George Orwell, called *Shooting an Elephant:*

> Afterwards, of course, there were endless discussions about the shooting of the elephant. The owner was furious, but he was only an Indian and could do nothing. Besides, legally I had done the right thing, for a mad elephant has to be killed, like a mad dog, if its owner fails to control it. Among the Europeans opinion was divided. The older men said I was right, the young men said it was a damn shame to shoot an elephant for killing a coolie, because an elephant was worth more than any damn Coringhee coolie. And afterwards I was very glad that the coolie had been killed; it put me legally in the right and it gave me a sufficient pretext for shooting the elephant. I often wondered whether any of the others grasped that I had done it solely to avoid looking a fool.

Directly or subtly comparing your own subject with the most dramatic endings in real life gives borrowed force to your own close. And that emotion *can* carry the reader past noticing that you have not actually answered some major question. Shakespeare, for instance, rarely lets us know exactly where he stands at the end of his tragedies, but the deaths have such shocking power that we feel, somehow, he has told us what he thinks. But he has done more than that, and less: he has convinced us of finality.

FAREWELL

Write a long goodbye to a factory or a machine, stating your considered opinion about it in terms that recall defeat or triumph—or simply farewell. Assume that you have already written ten pages on the subject.

Even when your writing stops, you may hope some part of it outlives the blank paper after the last period. For an ending resembles death. To survive it you need a lively soul.

So, at the end of your paper, do what you dream of doing in the moments before you die:

- Don't trail off or drag on.
- Deliver on your promises.
- Answer the questions you yourself raised.
- Recognize that this is the end: and time for a new beginning.

SOME LAST WORDS

I AM going to seek a great perhaps. Draw the curtain; the farce is played out. [François Rabelais.]

NOW comes the mystery. [Henry Ward Beecher.]

I AM ready at any time. Do not keep me waiting. [John Brown.]

I HAVE but one request to ask at my departure from this world—it is the charity of silence. Let there be no inscription on my tomb. Let no man write my epitaph. [Robert Emmet.]

30th DAY

After Words

In thinking about writing techniques, you have not lost any originality. In fact, you have probably discovered new ways or strengthened familiar ways of expressing your own views. The more aware you are of style, the more flexible your own writing can become, and the more you can say.

But does your style reflect your full personality? Can you express every shade of emotion, each turn of thought, exactly as it comes to mind? Does your writing seem a clear glass that lets your experience shine through, undistorted?

If not, you may want to go on learning.

Or do you still find it difficult to handle certain technical problems? Does organization baffle you? Do you yearn for a more logical tone? Or do you feel cramped, as if your emotions cannot get loose as you write? You may have a dim awareness of what you do well and what you avoid or botch. Read through pieces you wrote a year ago, as if you were studying someone else's work: spot the rough patches, and diagnose your own weaknesses. The cure?

You will learn a lot just from writing—and going on writing. If possible, get advice from editors or other writers, to determine which skills you need to polish. And at home, you can teach yourself new techniques by communing with authors you enjoy. I use the word *communing* by design: I mean more than simply reading them, though that can help. I mean: imagine you are with each author as she writes.

Second-guess her. Follow her as she invents each new word. Feel her breathing change as the sentences explode. By putting yourself in her place, you can acquire her skills—and more.

Think why you like certain authors. They express emotions you have, ideas you long to see in print; they reveal what you already knew, and they move parts of you that ordinary conversation skips over. Their skill impresses you because it is not empty: we admire not just techniques, but adroit self-revelation.

In communing with a writer we love, then, we absorb her half-conscious methods for bringing material into awareness. We guess at her aims. We sense how she felt as she wrote. And at this point we can begin to look at each word as a sign of a decision made. Each technique she used reflects a deliberate though not necessarily conscious choice. And as we watch these choices accumulate, we may notice that, together, they suggest an over-all strategy. The result of that strategy is style.

In order to express similar emotions, we may want to assimilate her style. We do not want to give up our own way of talking. But by submitting briefly to *her* style, we can make certain techniques our own.

By imitating, you can actually become more self-expressive. Imitation has a long, honorable history as a way of learning to write: Shakespeare did it, Chaucer did it, even the epic poets Virgil and Homer indulged in it.

How to imitate? Start with a quick analysis of your own writing. You might skim back through this book. Which techniques gave you most difficulty? What *general* problems still bother you? You might make a list of half a dozen things that bother you about your writing.

Then turn to your bookshelf. Which writers do you like, admire? Which do you wish you could outdo? Here, for instance, are some I like:

James Agee	Herman Melville
Sherwood Anderson	H. L. Mencken
W. H. Auden	John Milton
Amiri Baraka	Wright Morris
Samuel Butler	Flannery O'Connor
John Cage	George Orwell
Willa Cather	William Shakespeare
Raymond Chandler	George Bernard Shaw
Stephen Crane	Susan Sontag
William Faulkner	Lawrence Sterne
Henry Fielding	Henry David Thoreau
F. Scott Fitzgerald	James Thurber
Ben Franklin	Mark Twain
Robert Graves	Edith Wharton
Lillian Hellman	Eudora Welty
Ernest Hemingway	E. B. White
Thomas Macaulay	Malcolm X

Then flip the pages until you find a passage that moves you. See if the author is succeeding here at doing something you feel incompetent to do. Ponder the pervading tone: what kind of person does the author seem to be here? What attitudes come up?

And, word by word, what decisions has the author made? About handling descriptions? Contrasts? Logic? Endings?

When you can spell out each technique exactly, you are ready to begin an imitation. Depending on your interest, you can keep the form but substitute new words; you may maintain the emotional rhythm while talking about a new subject.

Or you might take apart the argument into its separate ideas, noting each down on a separate piece of paper. Put the original aside for a few days, then try to put the ideas back together in an appropriate order, to see how your organization fares.

Or, if you discover you actually hate the passage, parody it. Carry the superficial techniques too far; use them on an inappropriate subject or passion.

If you know another language, translate passages, stretching for the most appropriate American parallel, without sacrificing the pace and stance of the original author. Turning the same thought into different languages will make you more alert to the subtleties available in English.

IMITATION EXERCISE

In this book, or another, pick some passage you enjoy. First copy it verbatim, letting it move through you as you write. Imagine *you* are writing it:

_____

_____

_____

_____

_____

_____

_____

_____

_____

Now, is the author doing something you'd like to learn? Describe a few of the techniques and underline examples:

_____

_____

_____

_____

_____

Having defined what you hope to absorb, imitate the passage. Pick a somewhat different topic, but treat it in the same style:

_____

_____

_____

_____

To improve your writing to the point where it is easily and exactly right takes years and demands more than imitative exercise. So, don't stop working and growing. Growth demands and produces self-understanding, and the more you understand about yourself—your abilities, foolishness, strength, love—the more you'll be able to admit. In honesty lies excellence of writing.

The more you perceive, the more you'll have to say. And—a miracle—if you keep following your own impulses, you'll discover one day that these new realizations almost express themselves.

At that moment, you'll find you can write as casually as you breathe. You'll see you can simplify whatever you think—or turn it into a metaphor—so that when you address the reader, you sound like a friend, talking.

As you grow whole, then, your writing becomes unified and personal. Your style becomes your own.

Acknowledgments

For permission to use the selections reprinted in this book, the author is grateful to the following publishers and copyright holders:

DOUBLEDAY AND COMPANY, INC., for excerpts from *This Hallowed Ground,* by Bruce Catton. Copyright © 1955, 1956 by Bruce Catton. Reprinted by permission of Doubleday & Company, Inc. Excerpt from *The Shadow that Scares Me,* by Dick Gregory. Copyright © 1968 by Dick Gregory. Reprinted by permission of Doubleday & Company, Inc. Excerpt from *Pebble in the Sky,* by Isaac Asimov. Copyright © 1950 by Isaac Asimov. Reprinted by permission of Doubleday & Company, Inc.

ENCINO PRESS, for excerpts from *In a Narrow Grave,* by Larry McMurty. Copyright © 1970 by Larry McMurty. Reprinted by permission of Encino Press.

GROVE PRESS, INC., for excerpts from *Naked Lunch,* by William Burroughs. Copyright © 1959 by William Burroughs. Reprinted by permission of Grove Press, Inc.

HARCOURT BRACE JOVANOVICH, INC., for excerpts from *Beautiful Lofty People,* by Helen Bevington. Copyright © 1974 by Helen Bevington. Reprinted by permission of Harcourt Brace Jovanovich, Inc. Excerpt from *Technics and Civilization,* by Lewis Mumford. Copyright © 1934 by Lewis Mumford. Reprinted by permission of Harcourt Brace Jovanovich, Inc. Excerpt from *Shooting an Elephant,* by George Orwell. Copyright © 1950 by George Orwell. Reprinted by permission of Harcourt Brace Jovanovich, Inc. Excerpt from *A Room of One's Own,* by Virginia Woolf. Copyright © 1929 by Virginia Woolf. Reprinted by permission of Harcourt Brace Jovanovich, Inc.

HARPER AND ROW PUBLISHERS, INC., for excerpts from *Only Yesterday,* by Frederick Lewis Allen. Copyright © 1931 by Frederick Lewis Allen. Reprinted by permission of Harper and Row Publishers, Inc. Excerpt from *Simple and Direct,* by Jacques Barzun. Copyright © 1975 by Jacques Barzun. Reprinted by permission of Harper and Row Publishers, Inc. Excerpt from *The Art of Plain Talk,* by Rudolf Flesch. Copyright © 1951 by Rudolf Flesch. Reprinted by permission of Harper and Row Publishers, Inc. Excerpts from *Business Writing,* by J. Harold Janis and Howard R. Dressner. Copyright © 1956 by J. Harold Janis. Reprinted by permission of Harper and Row Publishers, Inc. Excerpt from *The Art of Making Sense,* by Lionel Ruby. Copyright © 1954 by Lionel Ruby. Reprinted with permission of Harper and Row Publishers, Inc. Excerpts from *The Insolent Chariots,* by John Keats. Copyright © 1958 by John Keats. Reprinted by permission of J.B. Lippincott Company, and Harper and Row Publishers, Inc.

HOUGHTON MIFFLIN COMPANY for an excerpt from *Unbought and Unbossed,* by Shirley Chisholm. Copyright © 1970 by Shirley Chisholm. Reprinted by permission of Houghton Mifflin Company. Excerpt from *Thoreau,* by Henry Seidel Canby. Copyright © 1939 by H.S. Canby. Reprinted by permission of Houghton Mifflin Company.

ILLINOIS STATE HISTORICAL SOCIETY, for excerpts from "Major James Austin Connolly's Letters to his Wife, 1862–1865," in *Transactions of the Illinois State Historical Society for the Year 1928*. Copyright © 1928 by Illinois State Historical Society. Reprinted by permission of the Illinois State Historical Society, Illinois State Historical Library, Old State Capitol, Springfield, IL 62708.

LITTLE BROWN AND COMPANY for excerpt from *All Quiet on the Western Front,* by Erich Maria Remarque. *Im Western Nichts Neues,* Copyright © 1928 by Ullstein, A.G.; Copyright renewed 1966, by Erich Maria Remarque. *All Quiet on the Western Front,* Copyright 1929, 1930 by Little Brown and Company. Copyright Renewed 1957, 1958 by Erich Maria Remarque. All Rights Reserved.

MACMILLAN PUBLISHING COMPANY, INC., for excerpt from *The Yogi and the Commissar,* by Arthur Koestler. Copyright © 1945 and renewed 1973 by Arthur Koestler. Reprinted by permission of Macmillan Publishing Company, Inc. Excerpt from *On Death and Dying,* by Elisabeth Kübler-Ross. Copyright © 1969 by Elisabeth Kübler-Ross. Reprinted by permission of Macmillan Publishing Company, Inc. Excerpt from *The Elements of Style,* Third Edition, by William Strunk, Jr., and E.B. White. Copyright © 1979 by Macmillan Publishing Company, Inc. Reprinted by permission of Macmillan Publishing Company, Inc.

MCGRAW-HILL BOOK COMPANY for excerpt from *What to Listen for in Music,* by Aaron Copland. Copyright © 1957 by Aaron Copland. For excerpt from *Soul on Ice,* by Eldridge Cleaver. Copyright © 1968 by Eldridge Cleaver. Reprinted by permission of McGraw-Hill Book Company.

NELSON-HALL PUBLISHERS for excerpts from *Johnny Deadline, Reporter,* by Bob Greene. Copyright © 1976 by Bob Greene. Reprinted by permission of Nelson-Hall Publishers, Chicago.

PENGUIN BOOKS, for excerpt from *Memory,* by Ian M.L. Hunter. Copyright © 1957 by Ian M.L. Hunter. Excerpt from *The Pillow Book of Sei Shonagon,* translated by Ivan Morris. Copyright © 1967 by Ivan Morris. Reprinted by permission of Penguin Books, Inc.

G.P. PUTNAM'S SONS for excerpts from *The Presidential Papers,* by Norman Mailer. Copyright © 1963 by Norman Mailer. Excerpts from *Advertisements for Myself,* by Norman Mailer. Copyright © 1959 by Norman Mailer.

RANDOM HOUSE, INC., for excerpt from *The Dyer's Hand,* by W. H. Auden. Copyright © 1956 by W. H. Auden. Excerpt from *The Random House Handbook,* by Frederick Crews. Copyright © 1974 by Random House, Inc. Excerpt from *A Mencken Chrestomathy,* by H. L. Mencken. Copyright © 1929 by Alfred A. Knopf, Inc., and renewed 1951 by August Mencken and The Mercantile Safe Deposit and Trust Company. Reprinted by permission of the publisher. Excerpt from "The Bear," by William Faulkner, in *Bear, Man and God,* edited by Francis Lee Utley, Lynn Z. Bloom, and Arthur F. Kinney. Copyright © 1971 by Random House, Inc. Reprinted by permission of the publisher. Excerpt from *Hiroshima,* by John Hersey. Copyright © 1946 by John Hersey. Reprinted by permission of the publisher. Excerpt from *The Death and Life of Great American Cities,* by Jane Jacobs. Copyright © 1961 by Jane Jacobs. Reprinted by permission of the publisher. Excerpt from *Working,* by Studs Terkel. Copyright © 1974 by Studs Terkel. Reprinted by permission of the publisher.

SKIP ROZIN for excerpt from "People of the Ruined Hills," published in *Au-*